D0170214

LITTLE LAMB
who made thee?

Books by Walter Wangerin Jr.

This Earthly Pilgrimage
The Book of God: The Bible as a Novel
Paul: A Novel
The Book of the Dun Cow
The Book of Sorrows
Preparing for Jesus
Reliving the Passion
Little Lamb, Who Made Thee?
The Manger Is Empty
Miz Lil and the Chronicles of Grace
Mourning into Dancing
The Orphean Passages
Ragman and Other Cries of Faith
Whole Prayer
In the Days of the Angels
As For Me and My House
The Crying for a Vision

For Children

Mary's First Christmas
Peter's First Easter
The Book of God for Children
Probity Jones and the Fear-Not Angel
Thistle
Potter
In the Beginning There Was No Sky
Angels and All Children
Water, Come Down
The Bedtime Rhyme
Swallowing the Golden Stone
Branta and the Golden Stone
Elisabeth and the Water Troll

LITTLE LAMB
who made thee?
A Book about Children and Parents

Walter Wangerin Jr.

ZONDERVAN™

GRAND RAPIDS, MICHIGAN 49530 USA

HarperSanFrancisco

A Division of HarperCollins*Publishers*

ZONDERVAN™

Little Lamb, Who Made Thee?
Copyright © 1993, 2003 by Walter Wangerin Jr.

Requests for information should be addressed to:
Zondervan, *Grand Rapids, Michigan 49530*

Library of Congress Cataloging-in-Publication Data

Wangerin, Walter
    Little lamb, who made thee? : a book about children and parents /
Walter Wangerin, Jr.
      p. cm.
    ISBN 0-310-40550-5
      1. Parenting—Religious aspects—Christianity   2. Wangerin, Walter.
    3. Parents—United States—Religious life.   I. Title.
    BV4529.W26 1993
    248.8'45—dc20   93-29995
                                                              CIP

Zondervan and HarperSanFrancisco edition ISBN 0-310-24826-4

All Scripture quotations, unless otherwise indicated, are taken from the *Revised Standard Version of the Bible,* copyright 1946, 1952, 1971 by the Division of Christian Education of the National Council of Churches of Christ in the USA. Used by permission

All rights reserved. No part of this publication may be reproduced, stored in a retrieval system, or transmitted in any form or by any means—electronic, mechanical, photocopy, recording, or any other—except for brief quotations in printed reviews, without the prior permission of the publisher.

Published in association with the literary agency of Alive Communications, Inc., 7680 Goddard Street, Suite 200, Colorado Springs, CO 80920.

Interior design by Michelle Espinoza

Printed in the United States of America

04 05 06 07 08 09 10 /❖ DC/ 10 9 8 7 6 5 4 3 2 1

CONTENTS

Part 3: The Parent of His Children

Part 4: The Parent of His Parents

Part 5: The Grandparent, Finally, of Many

Little Lamb, who made thee?
Dost thou know who made thee?
Gave thee life, and bid thee feed
By the stream and o'er the mead;
Gave thee clothing of delight,
Softest clothing, wooly, bright;
Gave thee such a tender voice,
Making all the vales rejoice?
Little Lamb, who made thee?
Dost thou know who made thee?

Little Lamb, I'll tell thee,
Little Lamb, I'll tell thee:
He is calléd by thy name,
For he calls himself a Lamb.
He is meek, and he is mild;
He became a little child.
I a child, and thou a lamb,
We are calléd by his name.
Little Lamb, God bless thee!
Little Lamb, God bless thee!

From *Songs of Innocence* by William Blake, 1789

1.
Tell me, girl: how is it you can rust
At three? The talk scrapes in your throat
Like hinges like to bust;
Idle joints lock and loose on a corrosive note;
Tiny flecks of oxide make your glances bold—
How is it, girl, that rust on you is just
Another brown more beautiful than gold?

2.
Jack Ketch, my sons have seen you!
On a tight October morning have
Seen you gibbet a million rattled leaves—
Each leaf a sinew
Popped, each fall a potter's field and grave—
Have seen you, Jack, and laughed at you!

3.
My sons heard rhythm in the falling leaves.
A rhythm's always an occasion for
The dance, so they danced! They danced like the poor;
They thumped it like berries in a metal pot,
Harrowed together a mountain of compost gore,
Excited the wind to a deeper declarative roar,
Went down with a laugh they had not laughed before—

4.
Make three angels in the snow,
Ageless, cold, and hollow;
Remind me once before you go
You, too, were here—then follow.

LET THE CHILDREN LAUGH and be glad.

O my dear, they haven't long before the world assaults them. Allow them genuine laughter now. Laugh *with them*, till tears run down your faces—till a memory of pure delight and precious relationship is established within them, indestructible, personal, and forever.

Soon enough they'll meet faces unreasonably enraged. Soon enough they'll be accused of things they did not do. Soon enough they will suffer guilt at the hands of powerful people who can't accept their own guilt and who must dump it, therefore, on the weak. In that day the children must be strengthened by self-confidence so they can resist the criticism of fools. But self-confidence begins in the experience of childhood.

So give your children (your grandchildren, your nieces and nephews, the dear ones, children of your neighbors and your community)—give them golden days, their own pure days, in which they are so clearly and dearly beloved that they believe in love and in their own particular worth when love shall seem in short supply hereafter. Give them laughter.

Observe each child with individual attention to learn what triggers the guileless laugh in each. Is it a story? A game? Certain family traditions? Excursions? Elaborate fantasies? Simple winks? What?

Do that thing.

Because the laughter that is so easy in childhood must echo its encouragement a long, long time. A lifetime.

But yesterday, even in my own community, these are the things I saw:

I saw a man walk toward me on the street, leading two children by the hand. His mouth was as straight as the slot of a mailbox, his eyes drawn tight as ticks. He wasn't looking at me. I greeted him. He did not answer. I greeted the children by name, the boy and the girl, and although these are our neighbors, I saw an instant and marvelous duplication: the children's mouths sucked in, as straight as mailbox slots; their eyes contracted, tiny and hard, like ticks. And I saw the cause of the change: the man, never yet glancing at me, had clamped their hands to silence.

Now, there may be many reasons why my neighbor would harden his heart against me. And some of these reasons may be reasonable. And perhaps it is not *un*reasonable that he should harden his children as well. But, while he has always carried his face like a cuttlefish, the boy had laughed quite blithely in my front yard the day before yesterday, and often the girl had made beautiful blushes of affectionate giggles when we spoke. They are changing. They are mimicking their elder.

And I saw a woman picking at her child, a baby no more than two years old. She was picking at him, pinching him, pushing him, prodding him forward as she walked and he trotted down the center of the mall. But the woman was scarcely aware of her own behavior. She was enjoying a conversation with another woman, friends out on a shopping trip.

But the baby couldn't maintain their adult pace. So she kept pushing his shoulders faster, faster—while his eyes grew huge with the fear of falling. Her eyes were fixed on her friend. Without looking at the kid, without ever losing the thread of her conversation, she interrupted herself to admonish him:

"Tad," she said—*poke, poke*—"keep moving."

"Go!" she snapped. *Poke!*

"Move it, dummy!" *Poke, poke, poke!*

Finally the woman stopped and, with her hand on her hip, actually looked at the kid. "Tad, what is the matter with you anyway?"

Well, he had sprawled face-forward on the ground. But he had gone down in perfect silence. Unto whom should he call for safety or support?

His mother was granting herself her own golden days—but at the expense of her son's. No one was laughing.

I saw a well-dressed man—a professional man, a man of success and genuine repute in our community—speaking in cool, indifferent tones to his daughter. His language was precise, articulate, intelligent, and devastating. No one could match his ironic contempt—least of all this adolescent. I think he thought he was being funny, that he was dealing with his daughter as an equal: two adults. Straight talk. No sentiment. No wishy-washy indirection. I think he thought his manner wonderfully restrained and civil; thus he could speak in public without embarrassment: "We communicate. We don't prevaricate. We tell the truth. We can take it." *Bang!*

But the truth he was imparting concerned her dress, her friends, her taste, and therefore herself. *Bang!* While his truth displayed his own self-confident intelligence and even his excellent, progressive method of parenting, it shot dead the child inside his daughter. An early death. Who was laughing then?

I heard inside a house two voices shouting. One belonged to an adult: "Brat! You never listen! I cook for you, I work for you, I bust my back and all I ask for in return is a little cooperation. Do I get it? No! What do I get from you? Nothing! Nothing! Oh, no, you don't! Don't you go rolling your eyes at me, baby brother—"

Two voices, but the one that belonged to the child was crying.

And I have heard the smack of human fury on human flesh.

And I have heard the laughter that children create on their own when their elders do not care. *That* laughter is bitter and sarcastic. That laughter declares with their parents: *Don't care. No, we don't care. No, nothing will get at us—*

And I've seen parents who, after seven years of not caring, suddenly rise up and fight on their child's behalf *against* the teachers, *against* some judgment of the educational or legal systems. These parents appear like heroes on the horizon, come to save their kids from systems which have, in fact, been trying to save the same children for the same seven years of parental neglect. This sudden, heroic passion on behalf of their kids is meant to prove parental love. It arrives too late. It looks too much like wrath to allow for laughter now. And these particular children ceased to laugh when they ceased to know their golden days—about seven years ago.

Sorrows such as these shall surely come—but surely, parents, not through us! Haven't we ourselves suffered the same abuses? Even as adults? And weren't they a misery more than *we* could stand? Isn't that motive enough to stop our tongues and stay our hands when we might wound our children? Do we need more?

Then hear this:

Children do not exist to please us. They are not *for* us at all. Rather, we exist for them—to protect them now and to prepare them for the future.

Who is given unto whom? Are children a gift to their elders? No—not till children are grown and their elders are older indeed. Then they are the gift of the fourth commandment, honoring hoary heads which have begun to feel past honor. But until then, it is we who are given, by God's parental mercy, to the children! And it is we who must give to the children—by lovely laughter, by laughter utterly free, and by the sheer joy from which such laughter springs—the lasting memory: *You are, you are, you are, my child, a marvelous work of God!*

THE CHILD OF HIS PARENTS

SPRING CLEANING

CURIOUSLY, I've never thanked my mother for cleanliness. But I should. And I do.

Here comes the spring of the year. Here comes an air so laden and loamy, breezes so sweet I want to weep. Here come some of the purest colors of the earth: jonquils of unsullied yellow, the rouge of the redbud like the red breath of the forest itself, the white of the petaled dogwood like explosions of pillows. Here comes that scent after thunderstorm that is so like the warm, clean scent of wind-dried bedsheets against my cheek.

It stormed last night. For several hours there was a full cannonade of thunder and the heavy rain—and then the air had a dark, sparkling quality in my nostrils. Intoxicating. The night streets shined. All the earth was washed. Today the soil is shrugging toward rebirth.

And all this reminds me of my mother.

One particular gift of hers to us was cleanliness. The experience of cleanliness, of becoming clean. We took it for granted; but it was a way of life, maternal virtue and holy consolation.

My mother kept cleaning, kept reclaiming territory by the act of cleaning it, kept redeeming her children therein.

And spring was always that fresh start of the faith and the hope in cleanliness, of the forgiveness of cleanliness, actually, since everything old and fusty *could* be eliminated, allowing the new to take its place—or better yet, the old itself could *be* the new again.

My, my, I haven't realized till now—sinking into a thoughtful old age—how dearly I loved spring cleaning.

Mom was happy, cleaning. She sang the winter away. She cracked old closures. Everything grievous and wrong and knotty and gritty and guilty was gone. Life returned, and sunlight and laughter and air.

She was a priest. This was her sacramental ritual. We children would wake in the early morning to a sudden bluster of wind through the house. Mom had thrown open all the windows upstairs and down, front and back, living room and our own bedrooms. The curtains blew in and clapped above us: *Get up! Get up! This is the Day of Atonement!*

We stumbled up to find that Mom had propped the front door open and the back door and the basement. We sailed through windy hallways.

Mother herself never paused the day long. She bound her hair in a bandanna blue with white polka dots; she wore weird pants called "pedal-pushers" and rubber gloves and a man's shirt and red canvas shoes with rubber soles: silent, swift, and terrible was she!

Rugs came up and were hung on lines outside for beatings. Her right arm got victories that day. Rugs coughed dark clouds into the yard, and then the hardwood floors were waxed with such power to such a marvelous shine that we, in sock-feet, slipped the surface, surfing. Clean is a feeling beneath your feet.

The curtains came down to be washed. The naked windows squeaked under Windex and newspaper. Mom's dust rag made the Venetian blinds clatter and complain. Bright light flooded the rooms. They seemed to inhale, these rooms, and so to enlarge themselves. Our house was growing. The furniture had to be moved back. In the huge, gleaming living room our voices echoed. Lo, we were new creatures, laughing with a louder sound and singing a sweeter treble than before.

Out with the old, then! Out with the bad. My mother was a purging white storm, focused and furious. Out with the sullen, germ-infested air, colds and flus and fevers. In with the spring! In with lily breezes!

In buckets Mom made elixirs of Spic and Span. She shook Old Dutch Cleanser on sinks as if it were a stick to scold. Throughout the house went ammonia smells, pine smells, soap smells, sudsy smells that canceled sweats and miasmas.

Winter clothes were washed and packed away. Summer wear appeared. Our very bodies lightened, brightened, beamed in newness and health.

I loved to be in my mother's house on such spring days.

Dresser drawers got new paper linings.

The closet hung straight and true.

By evening we ourselves were bathed, the dust of the day removed, leaving a creamy me.

And this, finally, was the finest comfort of the sacred day: that when I went to bed that night, I slipped my silver self between clean sheets. Sheets sun-dried and wind-softened and smoother to my tender flesh than four white petals of the dogwood tree. Delicious above me and below, blessing me and holding me at once: my mother's cleanliness. Such a sweet fastness of sheets declared the boy between them to be royalty for sure, chosen, holy, and beloved—the son of a wonderful queen.

Understand: the blessing embraced more than the house. The whole world seemed ordered and good in that day. My mother's feats of cleanliness persuaded me of universal kindness. I liked the world in which I dwelt, and I assumed it liked me, and I trusted it therefore.

Well, she sang when she cleaned. Her eyes flashed gladness. She had a plan, and she never doubted that she would accomplish it. Morning to night, I knew exactly where she was because her presence was a music, like birdsong, like the laughter of water.

What then? Why, then for me my mother *was* the springtime. She inaugurated it. She embodied it. She gave it her own peculiar and personal character. When she swept her right arm up, the firmament was made balmy and blue, and winter was over.

Never, never should children take so cosmic a gift for granted. "Cosmic," I say, because it defines our world for a while, and it teaches us whether to meet the real world hereafter with confidence and glad anticipation—or else with fears, anxieties, suspicions. We children inhabit twice the worlds our mothers make for us: first when that world is no wider than a house, a yard, a neighborhood, and then again when that world *is* the wide world—because her smaller world teaches us how to see and interpret the real world when we shall travel into it.

My mother made my infant world a clean, well-lighted place. Now, therefore, in spite of wretched evidence to the contrary, I continue to trust in the ultimate purity of God's universe.

My mother taught me the goodness of order and brightness. Now, therefore, I seek order in friendships and offer a bright unvarnished truth in return.

My mother assured me annually that newness has a right and a reality, that error can be forgiven, that the sinner can be reclaimed. In springtime she surrounded me with the immediate, primal light of God. Now, therefore, I trust renewal. Resurrection. Easter!

Surely, then, it is time to thank her.

With all my heart, Virginia, I thank you for the theology of your spring cleaning, the vernal sacrament. And how often, while we sat at worship in church, didn't you cock an eye at some smudge on my face? And how often didn't you spit on your handkerchief and with that most private cleanser, your personal scent, wipe the smudge away? Well, for that too, thank you.

I am washed within and without. I am myself the gift that you have given me, and all the world is the wrapping.

LOOKIN' FOR JESUS IN ALL THE WRONG PLACES

EARLY IN MY CHILDHOOD I suffered a spiritual crisis.

I can't remember now *how* early this was, but I was young enough to crawl beneath the church pews, small enough to be hauled back up by my mother one-handed, yet old enough to wish to see Jesus. I wanted to see Jesus with my own eyes. Ah, but I was also child enough to admit that I never truly had seen my Savior face-to-face. Never.

That was my crisis. Every Sunday everyone else who gathered for worship seemed so completely at ease that I was convinced they had seen God in his house. Everyone, that is, but me. They sang without distress. They prayed without regret. They nodded during sermons without a twitch of anguish, and I stared with envy into their peaceful faces. It was a party to which I alone had not been invited—in the Lord's own house, don't you see?

So who was it not inviting me?

I wanted desperately to see Christ Jesus strolling down some aisle in a robe and a rope and sandals, eating a sandwich, maybe, since I would catch him off guard, just being himself. I spent all the time between Sunday school and worship peeking into every room, the pastor's study, the roaring boiler room, seeking the signs of his presence. Nothing.

Do you think he'd hide from me? Well, I knew he knew his house better than I did. He could hide. Do you think I made him mad by some sin I couldn't even remember now? I promise, I tried with all my might to remember. But I couldn't remember one *that* bad. As soon as I thought of it, I was right ready to confess and be forgiven. Until then I tried to surprise the Lord in hiding.

During services I would slip down from the pew to the floor and peer among ankle-bones and pants-cuffs and shoe-laces. So then, that's when my mother hauled me one-handed high onto the pew-seat again and clapped me to her side with a grip incontrovertible.

She's a very strong woman, my mother. You don't cross her. Once a forest ranger said, "If you meet a bear, you give the bear the right-of-way. Get out of there." Yeah, but my mother could silence whole congregations with a single, searing, righteous glance—so when she *did* meet that bear she beat two pans together until the bear backed down. "Woof," said the she-bear, astonished. "Not with *my* kids!" snapped my mother, uncowed. A very strong woman. Therefore I could not drop to the floor any more during worship.

But my yearning, imprisoned, increased to something like a panic. *I wanted to see Jesus!*

The heart of a child is capable of great desolation and thereby of great cunning. The more I felt abandoned, the sharper became my baby wit, trying to figure where Jesus was hiding.

During one worship service, while the pastor stood facing a long wooden altar and chanting the liturgy, it dawned on me that the voice I heard was too rich to be his. This was a pale, thin preacher, but that chant charged the chancel like the King to Kings. Ha! Of course. The pastor was pretending. It was really *Jesus* who was chanting—Jesus, lying on his side in the altar-box, which was the size of a coffin, after all.

So, as soon as the final hymn was over and my mother's hard arm released me, I snuck forward, eyes ever on the altar to catch anyone else who might be sneaking away. Up the steps I went, right to the altar itself; and then I crept around to the side, and *YA-HA!*—I let out a loud shout to surprise the Lord in his tiny bedroom.

But nope. No Jesus. Nothing but dust and an old hymnal and a broken chair. And the angry arm of my mother, who hauled me home and caused me to sit on a bench for exactly the time of one more worship service.

The heart of a child can grow heavy with sorrow and loneliness. Why was Jesus avoiding me? Why did he take flight whenever I came near? Maybe it was my cowlick. I was not a pretty child. I knew that. Moon-faced, someone would say. Moony, generally. A daydreamer who frustrated folks who'd rather go faster. But—

But I really wanted to see Jesus.

Couldn't I see Jesus too?

Which room had I never checked? Was there any such room in the church? Was there somewhere all the rest of the saints made sure I didn't see?

Yes!

Oh, my, yes! Yes! My mother didn't know how helpful had been my time on the bench. It ended in pure inspiration. There was indeed one room into which I had never gone, nor ever so much as peeped—a sanctum of terrible mystery and terrible charm. It horrified me to think of actually entering the place. It tightened my loins and made me sweat all week long, every time I contemplated venturing that door. But I would. I wanted to see Jesus, and I was convinced that this room did above all rooms qualify for a Holy of Holies. Surely he was in that place where, if a boy came in unworthily, he would die on the spot.

And so it came to pass that on the following Sunday morning I wagered my entire life on chance that I knew where the Son of God lurked. That is to say, I risked my mother's wrath. During the sermon I flat slipped from the pew, ducked her reach, skipped down the aisle and tiptoed downstairs to The Dangerous Door, The Room of Sweet Folly and Holy Violence:

Breathlessly, I approached The Women's Bathroom.

The girls' *toilet,* you understand. Boys don't ever pass it without spasms of awe.

But I was determined. And the need had made me very bold. As bold as my mother.

I knocked. I nudged the door inward.

"Jesus? Are you in there, Jesus? Jesus?"

So then my life was over.

Nothing mattered any more. I was so hopeless when I returned to my mother in her pew that I felt no fear of punishment. She could do to me as she pleased, and it would mean absolutely nothing. Jesus wasn't in there. Mirrors and wide tables and weird smells were there; but the King of Creation did not dwell in the women's bathroom. Mom could kill me for all I cared. I had looked in the last place, and the last place was empty. There was no more.

Well, no, she didn't kill me. She froze me with a glance, blue-eyed and beautiful and severe: *Just wait, young man.* So what? She pointed to the front where the pastor in black was intoning: "This cup is the New Testament in my blood. . . ."

Blood. I guess she was indicating an ominous future for me. So what? What did I care?

"Do this in remembrance of me," said the gaunt, white, ghostly preacher, and then people began to move forward, pew by pew. They sang and they filed up the aisle.

My mother got up. She walked forward with them.

Surely I must have seen the ritual often before, but it never had had so curdling an effect on me before. I was stunned by what my mother proceeded to do.

She acted docile! In a strange humility this strong woman knelt down before the pastor. She bowed her head. And then—like a child, like a *baby*—she raised her face and let him feed her! Yo! My mother can handle me. My mother can handle the neighbors. My mother can handle black bears in the Rockies—and my mother can surely handle herself. Yet now, as meek as an infant, she accepted a cracker from the preacher's hand. Then he gave her a little drink, and she didn't even touch the cup with her hands. She sipped at his bidding. My mighty mother, brought so low! What power could have stricken her so?

Yet, when she came floating back down the aisle and into our pew, there was nothing of defeat in her face. There was a softness, rather. Pliability and private smiling. She was different.

She smelled different, too. She came in a cloud of peculiar sweetness, a rich red odor. When she sat and bowed her head to pray, I stuck my nose near her nose, whence came this scent of urgent mystery. She felt my nearness and drew back.

"Mama," I whispered, "what's that?"

"What's what?" she asked.

"That smell. What do I smell?"

"What I drank," she said.

I wanted to pull her jaw down and look into her throat. "No, but what *is* it?" I begged. "What's inside of you?"

"Oh, Wally," she shrugged, reaching for a hymnal, "that's Jesus. It's Jesus inside of me."

Jesus?

My mother started to sing the hymn. I stared at her. Her profile, her narrow nose, her perfectly even brow all suffused with a scent of bloody sweetness. *So that's where Jesus has been all along. In my mama!*

Who would have guessed that this was the room in the house of the Lord where the Lord most chose to dwell? In my mama. Strong woman, meek woman, a puzzle for sure. My mama.

Well, I clapped my own small self smack to her side, and I took her arm and wrapped it around me to be the closer to them I loved, and we sang, and I grinned. I beamed like sunlight.

And I know we sang a heroic *Nunc Dimittis:* "For mine eyes have seen thy salvation. . . ."

. . .in blood, in a rich red smell, in the heart of my mama.

Amen!

"NO, GRANDPA, WATCH MY MOUTH: CAFFY-CAPS!"

MY FATHER'S FATHER DIED YOUNG, almost four years younger than I am now. He left this earth at fifty-five. Last week Wednesday, I reached the fifty-eighth year of my own age.

Until bare months before his death, Reverend Walter C. Wangerin had been a Lutheran pastor in Grand Rapids, Michigan; but a hellishly high blood pressure so embrittled his body, so endangered his life, that the church council chose to lighten his load in spite of himself: they removed him from active pastoral service, hoping sincerely that the action would be temporary and beneficial. I visited Grandpa during that enforced vacation. To me he seemed no different than he had been before; he was the same man that had taught me one year earlier—at his dining room table on a drizzling afternoon—to pray as a mealtime prayer: "Oh, give thanks unto the Lord, for he is good, for his mercy endures forever." The heart was the same. And it's the heart the young child sees. He knows nothing of the explosions of blood pressure—and shortly after my departure, Rev. Walter C. Wangerin was admitted to the hospital. That was in February, 1948. On the thirteenth day of that month, in Chicago, Illinois, I was unwrapping presents given me for my fourth birthday. From my mother I received a set of Lincoln Logs wherewith I began to build whole villages. Grandpa, however, lying in his hospital bed, was coming to realize that this bed was his last bed.

As my Aunt Clara wrote me years and years later: "He lived less than two months after that trip."

That trip: Aunt Clara (my father's younger sister, whose warmer name was and is "Tante Teddy") had accompanied me on the train from Chicago's Union Station to Grand Rapids; she and I and

Grandpa and Grandma Wangerin then drove north together, to the Straits of Mackinac and the Upper Peninsula. This is the trip my aunt refers to. A most sacred journey, so it seems to me even yet today; for while we sailed the islands between Lakes Michigan and Huron, my grandfather bequeathed unto me the source and the name of our power over that ancient serpent who is called the Devil and Satan, the deceiver of the whole world.

When it was all done—the bequest, the trip and its return, our last night's sleep in the parsonage—Tante Teddy and I boarded the train in Grand Rapids and rode the rails home to Chicago, and my Grandpa died. I never saw him again.

So I exhort the elders among you, as a fellow elder and a witness of the sufferings of Christ, writes Peter the Apostle: *Tend the flock!* Grandpa Wangerin the Pastor tended his congregational flock, indeed. But Pastor Wangerin the Grandpa tended that single lamb, his oldest grandchild, just as well and yet more lovingly.

Peter defines the quality of such tending: *not by constraint, but willingly, not for shameful gain but eagerly, not as dominating those in your charge but being examples to the flock*: to that grandkid of swallowing eyes and a vulnerable heart.

Cast all your cares on him for he careth for you.

Be sober, be watchful.

Your adversary the devil prowls around like a roaring lion, seeking someone to devour. . . .

The train still belched smoke in those days. "Choo-choo," to the children.

The train still jerked its starts, because the engine wheels first spun hard and the chuffing grew frantic before metal caught metal, rim caught rail, and the unspeakable weight of the long train finally rolled slowly forward.

When we achieved speed in the sunlight, batting through the small towns, climbing swells of farmland, I kneeled on the seat and pressed my cheek to the window; I nearly gnawed the glass in my hungry desire to see the engine ahead, the great-hearted creature that whistled and roared and clickety-clacked the million little wheels beneath us, drawing us toward our destinies. But the engine stayed hidden in mystery, as impossible to see as to see my own face without a mirror.

And having arrived at the farther station, we stepped down from our coach, Tante Teddy and I, onto a long concrete island that ran between tracks and trains to a terminal I could not yet see. Noises, hootings, hissings, hollerings; the scents of metal heat and steam heat and the acrid coal smoke; dramatic changes of light and darkness—the great, grinding climate of the railroad station made an alien of me, small and profoundly cautious. Several tracks away an engine started up, sending a series of hard bangs down its entire length from the choking head to the caboose. Trains still concluded with cabooses in those days.

"Wally?" My aunt adjusted her glasses to see me the better. "Wally, are you all right?" She put forth her hand, and though I didn't take it—my arms being full of a cardboard carrying case— I produced a smile, and so we began to walk. We walked toward the distant terminal, passing along the carcass of our own particular train: the dining car, the lounge car, sleeping cars, the mail car, luggage car, coal tender. . . .

In those days a locomotive still relieved itself by blasting great clouds of steam from lower valves into the paths of oncoming boys, terrifying them.

"Yow!" I cried, jumping backward.

"Wait!" Tante Teddy started to reach for me, "It's okay—" Then, in mid-motion she reversed herself, turning back toward the steam-cloud and murmuring: "Dad?"

Behind the sound of hissing steam I, too, heard a low roll of gentle laughter, and I looked, and a form took shape in the cloud, and the features of a familiar face began to gather there, brown eyes grinning, silver hair enwrapping the sides of his head: Grandpa!

Grandpa Wangerin came striding out of the mist and into the clear air. Straightway he slipped his hands beneath my arms and lifted me. He swung me high above his face, then caught me and held me to himself, my case, my squeal, my bones and all.

And so in a twinkling we were through the terminal and in his car; and I beside him was no alien, was a citizen, after all; and the sunlit weather felt very good.

I knew Grandpa. I knew him by sight and by smell and by the texture of his chin and by the timbre of his voice when my ear received it straight through his bosom. Of *course* he was familiar to me: I remembered him with the mind of a four-year-old child, whose memories seem taken not from mere months passed, but rather from that perpetual and primal past in which God creates heavens and earths and gardens of savor and sweetness. And I trusted my grandpa, whose presence stretched backward forever, in whose presence I was at peace.

Forever and forever, then, Grandpa Wangerin had been a preacher, for I had seen him preach and that was my memory of him. He was noble in the pulpit, splendid in his black cassock and a surplice as white as his own silver hair. Grandpa had a baritone voice as comforting as the Paraclete. My father once told me that Grandpa had been offered a position with the Metropolitan Opera in New York City, but that he'd chosen to become a pastor instead. He did sing, of course. All his life long he sang in public, gladly—until the last years when his voice was torn ragged by a persistent cough, and even his preaching was disturbed. Dad said that Grandpa would always tuck two Ludens cough drops under his upper lip before he preached, hoping by the drizzle to suppress that cough until the sermon was done.

"But those cough drops destroyed his front teeth," Dad said, "and he lost them."

I don't remember that. I didn't see teeth-gaps. It's Grandpa's softly puckered smile I most recall.

Forever and forever, then, the man had smiled, his brown eyes steadfast and tender. He smiled when he shook hands at the church door after worship. He smiled with anticipation when, in the mornings, he crossed the lot between the parsonage and the parochial school in order to lead the children in a matins devotion. He smiled a private, unattended smile when, in the evenings after supper, he sat down in his study to inscribe the day in his diary. Grandpa had begun this practice already during the first days of the ministry. When one book was full, he closed it and began another, saving the whole series of books against some future reckoning. *My Grandpa writes books,* I thought to myself, watching him from the darkened doorway. *My Grandpa writes stories down on paper for people to read.* But the diary was not, in fact, a journal of his private thoughts. I doubt he ever considered his personal notions worthy of preservation, except as they served the greater good of the Gospel.

Just a few years ago I had the opportunity to see the diaries again for the first time. Yes, they told stories. Or perhaps it is truer to say that they only hinted at ten thousand stories while Grandpa repeated the same daily tale over and over: he was keeping the accounts of a common cleric of uncommon obedience. *Who then is the faithful and wise servant, whom his master has set over this household, to give them their food at the proper time?* My grandfather's diaries record plain facts and calculations: the dates and times of every visitation he made to members of his congregation, whether to serve communion, or to pray with them, or to visit folks who had fallen away. The diaries remember every appointment the pastor made and kept for marital counseling; for the weddings themselves; for baptisms and funerals. They note the Scripture lessons which he chose for occasional services. They are a record of Rev. Wangerin's external duties, not of the thoughts of his internal heart—except as the very keeping of every duty, preciously and faithfully, *was* his heart and his life, being his deepest vocation: *Blessed is that servant whom his master, when he comes, will find so doing.*

Yet, if I cannot now read my grandfather's heart in the words he left behind, I did and *could* read his heart in the lines written on his face while he sat in his study writing in the diaries. With a fearsome clarity I see the man's silver head bending lightly above his desk; the lamplight plays upward over his face, his smile appearing and vanishing by turns, unattended. I hear the short strokes of his fountain pen as he moves it across the page, bright in the darkish room. I think that Grandpa doesn't see me in the doorframe, watching. I am the oldest of his grandchildren. My name is Walter, too. I am named after him, though he is Walter Carl and I am Walter Martin, like my Dad. One day I will write just like Grandpa, words spilling from my fountain pen upon pages and pages. My face, too, will work like sunshine and clouds in skyborne exchanges; my face will show the sadness and the gladness of the stories I am writing. And, just like my Grandpa, I won't even be aware that these expressions are revealing my secret heart to someone beloved who is lurking nearby and watching me. But Grandpa screws the cap to his pen (the cap flashing a tiny white dot) and, rising, begins to sing in his slightly ragged baritone:

> *"Du lieber, heilger frommer Christ,*
> *der fur uns Kinder kommen ist . . ."*

Kinder! That means—as even then I know—"children"! Not looking at me, switching off the desk lamp, Grandpa is nevertheless singing about me. I can hardly stand it:

> *"damit wir sollen weiss und rein,*
> *und rechte Kinder Gottes sein."*

"Unfortunately," Tante Teddy wrote me forty-six years later, when I was fifty, "Dad discontinued writing in his diary early in February 1948, the day before he entered the hospital because of his soaring blood pressure. You and your grandma, I fear, did not realize that your grandpa's illness was terminal. He lived less than two months after that trip . . ."

That trip.

The car we drove in seemed full of talk to me. My young aunt was highly verbal then, as now she swims the English language, written or spoken, as smoothly as a porpoise. Into most pauses she introduced sentences of endless delight.

Grandpa himself commented on every passing thing: "The solid line's to keep us in our places; the broken lines allow us to scoot." And: "Look, Wally—windmills!" He read all the roadside signs out loud: "Burma Shave!" with a smiling triumph. And sometimes he broke into song. Hymns, actually. *Wachet Auf.* The bass lines of German chorales. "Come, *mein Enkelsohn,*" he urged. "Sing with me!"

Once, while driving between the tall pines, Grandpa took his eyes from the road and squinted sententiously at the side of my head. "*Kinderschrecke!*" he whispered, not looking back to the road: "*Mir gruselt auf Kinderschrecke. Dir auch?*"

And I nearly yipped that my formal, controlled, obedient Grandfather kept his eyes fixed on me, allowing the car to drive itself.

Grandma raised a harsh complaint.

But "*Dir auch?*" Grandpa repeated, looking at me. *You, too?*

"Yes, yes, yes, yes," I said, in order to save us alive. Yes to whatever quiz the man was giving me.

Well, well: that quick flash of wickedness passing again from his face, the Reverend Walter C. Wangerin lifted his eyes once again to the road, smiling gravely and uttering his next words with a pulpit clarity: "Bogeymen give my grandson the creeps. Just as they do me. My grandson and me, why, we are the same. Two peas in a pod."

Apart from her various admonitions, I remember my grandmother chiefly by her silences and the marvelous revolvements of hair piled upon her head.

I must have lent my own chatter to the talk as we drove. The car and my relatives invited it.

And then, at the peak of our journey, the four of us were gathered on the deck of a sightseeing boat, sailing from island to island, nudging near the shores. It was a flat, canopied vessel, set with rows of chairs like pews on the deck. It was populated by people as white-haired as my Grandfather, though older than he was, truly, and wrinkled and grateful to be sitting beneath a canvas shade. I recall two tin speakers attached to the forward wall, crackling now and again with an impossible monologue. I knew that they were issuing

words, that someone somewhere was saying something; but I had
no idea *what* was being said.

Grandpa drew me near to him and murmured translations for
my sake, and then I understood that a guide was describing the
sights to be seen ashore; and as Grandpa pointed his finger, I too
began to see the sights. Most of them. Not all of them.

To me the scene spread all around was an Eden, raw wood,
creation undiscovered: tall trees and a vernal undergrowth, the
sudden sweep of eagles in the air, wheeling on a soundless wing.
And the air itself was a sun-splintered crystal, a breathless, dimen-
sioned clarity. And through the trees strong rays shone slantwise
earthward, splashing the needles and the foliage below.

The speakers crackled, *There! Do you see—?* But I lost the next
words.

Grandpa translated, "Two deer on that spit of land," he said,
pointing. "See them, Wally?"

"No." No, I couldn't see them, but was suddenly filled with desire.

"Their heads are down. They're feeding."

"Grandpa, no! I *don't* see the deer."

"Okay," he said. "Come."

And so it was that Grandpa led me to the very back of the boat.
He put his hands beneath my arms and lifted me up. But the
canopy covered the entire deck; so Grandpa leaned backward over
the stern and swung me out, bodily, above the boil of propeller-
churned water. My feet dangled down. I regarded the white confusion some ten feet below, but I did so only glancingly, without
fear, because Grandpa's hands were gripped around my chest, and
Grandpa himself was raising me higher and higher until I could
with my own eyes see over the canopy.

"Do you see the deer," he called.

And I looked. And, yes! Yes, I saw the two deer, both of them,
one with its head bent down in a spray of green fern, the other with
its head lifted up and looking directly back at me.

"Yes, Grandpa! I see the deers. I see two deers."

Tend the flock, not by constraint but willingly, not dominating those
in your charge. . . .

And so I hung above my death, and I was not afraid. In fact, I was sweetly oblivious of every emergent danger—not, mind you, because the dangers were not real, nor yet because I could not know them. In a moment I'll show you how desperately susceptible the boy at four could be to peril and its mortal terrors. No, I was oblivious because I was experiencing—was even in that moment *receiving*—my Grandfather Wangerin's sacred bequest: power over Satan and every deadly evil.

But it's a child's manner first to experience some new thing with a mindless subjectivity—and only later to learn the thing, to think *about* it with an analytic objectivity. On the boat I received and had what I did not know I had. It was only later, on the railroad train as it hurtled home to Chicago, that I learned what had been bequeathed me, and whence it was and how to call it by name.

I sat by the window on the right side of the coach.

Again, I was suffering the hungry desire actually to see the steam locomotive that pulled us forward—to see it, you understand, *while* it was active and living, belching smoke and directly affecting me by its monstrous speed.

I climbed to kneeling on my seat. I pressed my right cheek against the glass and, one-eyed, peered ahead.

It was late afternoon. The sun, standing off my side of the train, had descended nearly to the horizon, giving the country fields and forests a golden hue, as if the trees and the chopped corn glowed with their own sanguinity.

And then the miracle began to happen so reasonably that I in my heart said, *Of course! This is exactly the way it always happens.*

The long train began to curve into a lazy right-hand turn. I peered, and saw a flattened black shape racing in the forefront. The engine! Bending into my view! And soon I saw the tight blow of smoke into the streaming air, and the cloud torn backward, developing over the engine—and then the stretch of that dark metallic snout, and yes! Yes! There it was! There was the force itself, the cause of my rocking here on my seat, the thunderous muscle that even now was drawing cars and cars and a thousand people round a big bend to Chicago.

Almost I turned to tell my aunt of the wonder—but just then the engine's window flared with a bloody red reflected sunlight. I gasped, terrified. To my child's mind, this was a living, angry, glaring *eye*. And all at once I knew the danger: that our engine was the iron head of a serpent, and the entire train was its body, and all we inside the train were in the serpent's belly, and now the serpent was staring straight back at me as if it *knew* that I knew the horror which no one else had realized.

Do not dismiss this experience of cosmic discernment as the foolish imaginings of a child! It is at the promptings of such symbols as these that the child leaps past the slow processes of logic and in an instant understands the presence and the grandeur of wickedness in the world.

Mute, too terrified to let *anyone* know (and so to suffer) the truth that had been imparted to me, I bore alone the conviction that we had been consumed by evil. The serpent, that devil wandering the earth seeking someone to devour, had devoured us. . . .

Grandpa? Grandpa Wangerin?

Spontaneously I called to him in my mind. I did it before I knew that I was doing it: *Grandpa, why aren't you here?*

And then with a spiritual swiftness I learned. I held in my two separate hands these two separate experiences and all in a wordless flash considered their differences.

I am afraid. Because Grandpa is not here.

It was that simple. Grandpa was back in Grand Rapids.

But the very thought, the remembering of the boat and the dangers then and the fact that I was *not* then afraid because my Grandpa's hands then bore me up—that very thought, I say, brought ease into my situation now. Not that Grandpa had come upon the wings of my own memory. No. But rather that Grandpa had bequeathed me something that followed me then and ever. The source of our power over evil was in us. In *us*, the being together, you see, even when we were not together. And this was the name of that wonder: Love.

I sat down on the train seat. I kept my own counsel. I held my breath until we made Chicago. But I had begun to trust that we *would* make Chicago. And when we did, Grandpa's bequest had become a tangible thing within my breast.

And now that I am a man—and a grandfather too, in my own right—I can declare as a sacred fact, that this manner of being together outlasts every trip we take, even the final journey into death.

Shortly before my Tante Teddy wrote me her remembering letter, I had published parts of the story as you've read it above. She read those parts as well and dearly wanted to add several things and to correct several things.

I recall, she wrote, *that you and your grandpa had some pretty extensive conversations throughout that trip. Grandpa loved to explain how things worked. Grandpa said, "Look, there's a windmill," and you, Wally, four years old, you said, "I call them caffy-caps." Apparently Grandpa didn't repeat your word correctly, because you said, "No, Grandpa, watch my mouth: caffy-caps."*

The boat ride was indeed spectacular. My 22-year-old self was not into scenic appreciation, but I remember being awestruck by the lush virgin timber, the rare wildlife up close and personal, the rushing, gorgeous waters of the river. And I was right there next to your Grandpa when he lifted you out over the railing to see the deer, with your Grandma fretfully admonishing behind us, "Oh, Walter, be careful!"

I don't recall all the towns we saw.

Unfortunately, Dad discontinued writing in his diary early in February 1948, the day before he entered the hospital because of his soaring blood pressure. So what's the tribute?

He lived less than two months after that trip, but oh, what warmth and joy and contentment you showered upon those last two months! You recognize so eloquently his love for you, Wally, dear Wally. You gave as good as you got. For the rest of his life your Grandpa basked in your love and your trust and your irresistible four-year-old wonder at the world around you. Whenever he'd seem in pain or feeling sad during my hospital visits, I would mention a few catch-words from the Upper Peninsula trip, and he'd be instantly diverted to those happy memories and ultimately to peace of mind and of soul.

Thank you for making that visit with me and for doing so much to enrich your Grandpa's life.

It becomes even more evident, then, how in the being together we constitute a power against the greatest evils of this existence, Satan and desolation. And death. And the name of such wondrous being together even when we are no longer together is itself tough, enduring, and scarcely sentimental: Love.

In a postscript Tante Teddy concludes her letter:

I submit reluctantly to your poetic editorial license, but ding-dong it, Wally! There's no way I'd let an iron-headed serpent swallow my nephew down!

MY SHIELD AND
PORTION BE

IN THOSE DAYS HOMESICKNESS seemed to curl in me like a little creature deep in my bowels. When it stirred, I suffered a sweet abdominal pain, like having to go to the bathroom. If it only stirred and stayed put, well, then I was okay. No one needed to know what was going on inside me. But if my homesickness grew worse and worse, that creature seemed to climb through my stomach into my chest. In the chest it was a suffocation, and I would puff and puff and suck air, and this would look like sobbing, but I wasn't sobbing, exactly. No, I was not crying. I was fighting the tears. I had not yet lost control.

But when the homesickness rose all the way into my throat, then it was a plain pain at the root of my tongue, and *then* I was crying. Then my sobs were huge gulps. And then almost nothing could console me, and everyone knew there was a problem with Wally.

I was often homesick, is how I understood the process so well.

But I had good reason to be.

I feared death. There was a lot of death around me.

Well—how does a kid know, when he has left behind him his home and his mother, his brothers and everything he loves, that they might not die while he is away? He wouldn't be there to save them in the event of disaster—and a kid just at the age of entering school can conceive of countless disasters.

Or who's to say the kid himself won't die away from home? And who would be there to hug him then, when his mother's absent?

Or, worst of all: what if his family just didn't care? What if they forgot the kid while he was gone? What if they finally decided that he was just too much trouble to put up with, so they all packed and moved away and he would find a shining empty house at his return?

36

Well, whom would he go to *then* for help? The principal? Principals don't love small boys. He'd have to live on his own, forever sad that the thing he had feared actually happened exactly as he feared it.

Or what if he got lost on the way home? His mother would just cry her eyes out, so sorry, so sorry to lose her eldest, most precious son. So how could the boy live with himself, imagining the great grief he had caused his dear mother?

You see? All this is death. Different kinds of dying. But any one was a possibility.

That's why, on the first day of kindergarten, surrounded by strangers of various levels of confidence, the boy put his head down on the floor and cried. He feared death, and it made him unspeakably homesick.

That's why, when he was left with his Aunt Erna in St. Louis while his mother was in Chicago, he cried for two days together.

And again, the first day of first grade, he made it almost to lunch, but not all the way, and he put his head down on his desk, and the rest of the people looked at him. *Something's wrong with Wally.*

Yep. Something. The little creature of sorrow was clawing raw the back of his throat; his tummy felt completely empty, but his face was all full of sadness.

Death. He always lost, the kid did, when confronted with this lonely skull-bone of abandonment and death. But how could he defeat it? He was just a kid, a little one, weak, not strong. Not strong at all.

Yet that's exactly what my mother asked of me: "Oh, come on, Wally! Are you little or big?" she demanded, and I knew the answer she wanted, and I knew the truth. "Are you weak or strong?" she said.

I sighed and whispered, "Strong."

"Right!" she said. "Let's go."

Go our dusty ways to death, lonely, lonely on the way.

In the spring of my second-grade year, several months before the school term concluded, my whole family moved from Chicago,

Illinois, to Grand Forks, North Dakota. My father had accepted a call to serve Immanuel Lutheran Church as its pastor. This church also maintained a parochial school, eight grades and kindergarten, though classes had to double up in rooms, one teacher taking several.

This meant that a little kid might meet some very old kids even in his classroom.

So, then, here we were in a completely new environment, a new neighborhood in which every face was strange, and even a new house, a huge house, a three-story house that made odd sounds in the night, keeping me awake with wondering.

So, then, I was completely unprepared for my mother's plans for me. *Surely,* I thought, *in the midst of so foreign a territory we need not increase the strain by dividing the family just now.* Surely she knew that the potentiality of death at separation had just shot up to plague levels.

They told me that tornadoes could come straight up from South Dakota and hit Grand Forks directly on the nose, just like that. They said, "Watch out!"

But my mother said, "I think you ought to go to school."

I said, "School's almost over for the year."

She said, "All the better to go now. Meet classmates now and they'll be your friends by next year."

I was aghast. Already now, even at this distant early stage, I felt the small creature stirring in the cradle of my loins. Sweet pain.

I said, "What about the tornadoes?"

She said, "What *about* tornadoes?"

"They'll probably come while I'm gone."

"Oh, Wally, that's utterly silly."

"I don't think so."

"Well, you don't know what's best. The sooner the better."

I said, "I don't feel very well."

She said, "Oh, come on, Wally! Are you little or big? What will your brothers think of you?"

So, then, in spite of the clear probability of death by disaster, my mother prevailed. She's a strong woman.

So, then: three of us drove on the following morning to the white wooden, two-story structure, Immanuel Lutheran School.

Three of us. My mother, myself, and the creature deep within me, tickling the lower parts, stirring, stirring, threatening. Homesickness. But I said I wouldn't cry.

Mom took my hand and led me from the car into the building, up the stairs, and into a classroom. She introduced me to Miss Augustine, who was to be my teacher. This woman was beautiful beyond description, lithe and soft and tall, but she was a teacher. I hoped she would forgive me, but teachers by nature can be frightening, and even the smells were strange in this room, and the sunlight seemed cold and northerly and unkind. I felt a serious spasm of homesickness below my stomach. Therefore, as soon as Mom and Miss Augustine fell to talking together I slipped out of the room, down the stairs, out the door, and into the car, front seat. There I sat and waited for Mom to come back.

I persuaded myself that my mother would be delighted by my decision, as relieved as I was to find that I would be going home with her after all today.

Well—no.

When she found me in the car, my mother opened the passenger door, put her hand on her hip, and demanded, "What's this? What's the matter with you? Wally, Wally, are you little or big? Are you weak or are you strong?"

I sighed and whispered, "Strong."

"Right! Let's go."

I huffed a little. I puffed a little. Things were swelling in my chest.

I sat in the back with the W's. Wangerin. A kid named Corky Zimbrick sat behind me.

I didn't talk. I didn't move. My face was already warm. My mother had driven away some time ago. I was alone. Danger zone. Homesickness had made itself felt in the regions of my chest. I *had* to hold completely still.

The beautiful Miss Augustine was saying something, teaching something to someone—but which class it was, mine or those older than me, I didn't know. All sound was like waterfall in my ears: a roaring.

Corky Zimbrick whispered in my ear, "Who are you? Are you the preacher's kid?"

Oh no, I was known! Someone actually knew me. It was like being snatched from hiding. I started puffing and puffing, sucking huge chestfuls of air. Homesickness was coming higher, almost too high to be controlled.

I raised my hand.

Miss Augustine saw it immediately. Extraordinary woman! Without a word she nodded full recognition of my request and permission thereto.

I got up and rushed out of the classroom, down the hall to the bathroom. I unzipped and stood up to the urinal, pretending to pee. All I wanted was to be alone for a while, to control the great grief rising within me—to stand perfectly still, to concentrate my energy on not crying. I said I was not going to cry this time.

Those were big urinals in those days. Big as a kid. Big as a closet. Intimidating. You stared straight forward at concave porcelain that seemed to be waiting for proof you belonged there.

Suddenly the door behind me banged open. With thunderous energy there entered an eighth-grade teenager, huge fellow. He recognized me.

"Hey, Wally," he shouted, bellying up to the urinal beside mine.

I recognized him, too, and I burned to be in his presence. This was Dicky Affeldt, the principal's oldest son. This was a man of the world, a wild and sinful sort. Just last Sunday I saw him in a deserted Sunday school room with an eighth-grade woman named Marcia. She had so many freckles all over her body that even her eyes were flecked with freckles. Well, Dicky Affeldt had her bent backward over a utility table and was kissing her on her freckled lips. And she laughed! She had actually laughed.

He said, "Hey, Wally," but I didn't answer him. I stepped closer to the urinal to hide that I was not peeing.

He started to whistle, making a torrent against the porcelain. Then he looked at me. "What color's yours?" he asked.

I hoped he didn't mean what I thought he meant. This was becoming as frightening as I expected the world to be.

"What color's your pee?" said Dicky Affeldt. "Mine's clear," he said. "That happens when I drink lots of water."

Yep! Yep! He meant what I thought he meant. I was in the world, all right: treacherous, immoral, dirty, strange, and dangerous.

I zipped and raced out of there before I became the more involved. My mother should *know* what obscenities I had to deal with here.

Back in the classroom, back at my desk, I sat violently still, biting my teeth together as hard as I could. That little creature, homesickness and horror, had crept higher on account of the lewdness of Dicky Affeldt. It was nearly throat-high. It was almost uncontrollable. I breathed deeply, deeply, blowing air out at the nose, staring directly at the bottom left-hand star on the American flag— not crying. I said that I would not cry.

But then the worst thing happened, and I lost it.

They sang a hymn.

Hymns'll kill you.

All the kids in the classroom started to sing, "Blest be the tie that binds/Our hearts in Christian love—," and homesickness clogged my throat and squirted out my eyes. I burst into tears, sobbing, sobbing. I put my head down on the desk and tried at least to cry quietly. But I was crying, now. Nothing could stop it or console me. Nothing.

Miss Augustine called for recess. Kids began to rush outside.

"What's the matter with him? Isn't he coming?"

"Never mind," said Miss Augustine. "Never you mind, Corky Z."

So, then it was altogether still in the room. So I allowed some boo-hoos, some genuine shuddering sobs, all with my head down on my arms, down on the desktop.

Suddenly I heard humming beside me.

I peeped out underneath my arm and saw Miss Augustine sitting at the desk across the aisle from mine. She was huge in the little seat.

She was grading papers. She glanced at me. Straightway I covered my face again.

"Walter Martin?" she said in soft voice. "Walter Martin, do you mind if I sit here?"

I shook my head.

"Oh, thank you," she said. "Sometimes I like to sit here when I do my work."

She began to hum again. Soon the humming turned into a little song, with words: *Jesus loves me, this I know—*

But then, in the middle of a line, she stopped. "Walter Martin?" she said. "Walter Martin, do you mind if I sing?"

I shook my head.

"Thank you," she said. "Sometimes I like to sing when I work."

—for the Bible tells me so—

Then she said, "Walter Martin, do you know this song?"

I nodded. I did. I had learned it last summer.

She said, "Well, then, do you want to sing it with me?"

Forever and ever I will recall with admiration that Miss Augustine was not offended when I shook my head, meaning no. It was in this moment that I began to love my teacher. Somebody else might have gotten mad because I wouldn't sing with her. But Miss Augustine, in her soft voice, said, "Oh, that's right. Little boys can't sing when they're crying, can they?"

She knew that she was not the problem, that I was.

She said, "Well, but do you think we could shout the song together?"

So then the children of Immanuel Lutheran School who were playing on the playground for recess heard two voices roaring through the windows, one fully as loud as the other:

"JESUS LOVES ME, THIS I KNOW! FOR THE BIBLE TELLS ME SO—" And I screamed as loud as I could, blowing the creature of homesickness out of my throat, dispelling sorrows and fears and mournings together:

LITTLE ONES TO HIM BELONG!

THEY ARE *WEAK,*

BUT *HE* IS STRONG.

YES!
JESUS LOVES ME. YES—
Yes, yes, yes. Jesus loves me. Yes.

Ah, Miss Augustine, teacher of natural skill and native insight into a kid's horrific fears: together we met death; we outfaced that specter together; and never have I forgotten the triumph. Once, while still I was young, death did not defeat me, but by a brazen shout and an expression of perfect faith, death itself—and home-sickness too—was whipped. *Whupped!*

You shaped a boy, and forty years passed, and the boy became a man, and even today I declare the simple truth of *who* is strong after all, and who is weak, and in whose weakness power is made perfect.

Dear teacher, I heard recently that your smile is lopsided because a stroke destroyed the strength on one side of your face. Do you still shout your faith in the time of trial? The signs of dying? I do.

Last month my friend and my doctor, Stephen Ferguson, died suddenly and altogether too soon, leaving behind him two young children. No, three: his death reduced me to a child again. Home-sickness stormed in me. I preached his funeral sermon—and I would have wept then except that first I had gone striding through a deep wood, roaring at the top of my lungs:

> JESUS LOVES ME, HE WHO DIED,
> HEAVEN'S GATES TO OPEN WIDE;
> HE WILL WASH AWAY MY SIN,
> LET HIS LITTLE CHILD COME IN.
> YES, JESUS LOVES ME!
> YES, JESUS LOVES ME.
> YES, JESUS LOVES ME—
> THE BIBLE TELLS ME SO.

'TWAS GRACE THAT TAUGHT MY HEART TO FEAR

IN THE SUMMER OF my seventh year I found an electrical cord in the kitchen and was immediately dazzled by its potential for wild, destructive power.

My mother was in the backyard mowing grass. She used a pushmower in those days, a clattering metal machine whose blades spun only when one drove the wheels forward with fierce energy. My mother possessed such energy. Brave, she was, strong enough to hit a softball farther than my father could, strong enough to punish a child with such rectitude he knew he'd met the forehead of the Deity. Whatever he'd done before she chastised him he would never do again. God had spoken in the arm of a mortal woman.

Clunk-whirrrr, went the mower outside. Thus I heard the power of her matriarchal arms: *Clunk-whirrrr! Whirrrr!*

Why I happened to be alone, I don't remember. I was the oldest of five and should have been baby-sitting. Dad was at church. Mom was busy. The children were my responsibility. Yet the kitchen was altogether mine, and I was alone.

And there was that black electrical cord. I drew it out of its drawer and pinched it as you pinch a serpent's neck, just behind the plug. The blinkless head. Two prongs like venomous fangs would strike and bite any socket in the wall.

The tail of the cord was a plume of naked copper wiring. The cord attached to nothing.

So, if I stuck this plug in a socket, there in the mild reddish metal would be such violent force that it could kill at a touch. *Yow!*

Heaven and earth could collide at the command of a seven-year-old boy. My tummy tightened at the thought.

Well, and I knew the potency of electrical outlets. At the age of four I had managed to stick my right thumb into a living-room socket and had suffered a rapid, pulsing shock. It snapped my teeth shut and threw me backward across the room. My mother greased my poor thumb with butter, her healing of all horrors.

But here was a serpent that could suck juice from the wall and hold it in the bright ends of its tail—for *me! For* me rather than against me. This snake could strike with true authority where *I* willed it. I myself could hold a cobra of inestimable damage in my own two hands—

—if only I would, you know, plug it in—

Clunk-whirrrr! My mother labored in vigorous oblivion outside. I was alone. Nothing stopped me from arming my rattler. So I did. I thrust the teeth of this *Blitzschlange* into the socket by the refrigerator and stood back, pulling the cord out to length, staring at the copper scream of tail beneath my face—so close, so close to disaster! I began to grin. I could scarcely breathe because of my audacity.

But what good is the possession of power unless there's some evidence of it?

I began to wave my hand back and forth, swinging the snake's tail left and right, up and down in front of me. But nothing happened, of course. So I increased the speed, giggling, panting. Oh, I was scaring myself! Soon I was whirling the cord above my head like a lariat, barking a harsh, frightened laughter on account of such daring. I was so rash. Such a wild kid—

Suddenly, *crack-BOOM!* Copper wires struck the white refrigerator; yellow flame flashed forth; an explosion sent me backward, snatching the snake from its socket, and throwing me down on my butt against the far wall.

I held my breath a moment and surveyed the situation. I was alive. Not wounded. I had dribbled a little in my pants, but that dark shadow would pass. Here was the black cord dead across my legs. I—

Oh, no! Oh, *no!* Suddenly I saw that the refrigerator door had been scorched black by my sin. That yellow flash had burned white metal to a filthy char! Oh, no!

Clunk-whirrrr! Mama, what are you going to do to me when you see this? *Clunk-whirrrr! Whirrrr!* I began to whimper. I dribbled a little more. Now I felt the fear I had not felt before, my mother being more deadly than a whole nest of serpents. My life was in jeopardy. Before nightfall I would be dead.

Clunk-whirrrr!

Well, then this wet child arose from the kitchen floor and minced toward the refrigerator and put forth his thumb and touched the black patch of his personal wickedness—and lo! Where he touched, he wiped it clean!

"Jesus, Jesus, thank you!" This child experienced a sudden honey-spurt of gratitude in all his muscles, so that he trembled and he lifted up his heart unto the Lord in joy. Black patches from electrical shocks can be erased after all! Sins and error can be canceled!

He ran for a rag and rubbed the mark away altogether, rubbed the white door white again, rubbed iniquity clean.

And so it was that at seven I did not die, neither from the bite of the serpent (which could have killed me, body and soul) nor from the wrath of my mother (which, far from desiring my death, desired my life, loving with an angry love, a dreadful love, a mother love alone).

I have since myself become an adult. And a father. A man who prays for his children with loud cries and tears, since his own experience has shown him how closely all children do creep toward the dangers. They could die! Even my beloved sons and daughters, unprotected by my love when I am outside and oblivious, could by their own hand die!

I pray: *O Lord God, save the children from danger, from the cunning of the Evil One, and from the disasters of their own stupidity!*

How often have they covered some sin to keep it from me?—my child, my children, in the fond notion that they could save their lives thereby, though it is the sin itself that can kill them!

Christ, let terror check them!

I love my children. Even in my sometime anger—especially then— I love them and beg your mercy upon them. Amen. Amen.

AND GRACE MY
FEARS RELIEVED

FIRST OF ALL THE LOVE of God is a terrible thing. It begins by revealing unto us such treacheries and threats in the world that we know we must die soon—and until then (we are sure) we shall live in continual terror of the end to come.

The first act of divine love is to persuade us of the reality of death. We shudder and doubt that this can *be* love. We hate the messenger. We loathe such lovers. But it is a dear, necessary act nonetheless, because without it the second act of God's love would be altogether meaningless to us.

The second act is mercy. An absurdity of mercy. It is that God himself enters the same reality he first revealed unto us; he bows down and joins us under the same threat of death—and those whom he taught to fear he leads to safety. But those who do not fear do not follow. See? We had to suffer extremest fright in order to know our extreme need.

We who are under death must admit the peril; we have no other choice—except to die. Except to die.

But God, who exists above death, who knows no need at all, had the choice which we did not have. If, then, he emptied himself of power and humbled himself to death—even to death on a cross— this was purely an act of mercy on our behalf.

Then who can measure the love of God, to be thrice sacrificed: first, to be despised for declaring the terrible truth; second, to descend by choice into this treacherous and transient world; third, to save us by dying indeed the death he had revealed, dying it in our stead? Or whereto shall we liken so violent, valiant, and near an approach of the kingdom of heaven unto us?

Well—

～

The coming of the kingdom is like the coming of my father to my brothers and me when we sat fishing, blithely fishing, from a ledge twelve feet above the water in a stony cove in Glacier National Park.

In that year of sudden awakening, 1954, I was ten. My brothers, grinning idiots all (for that they followed a fool) were, in descending order, nine and seven and six.

Just before our trip west, I had furnished myself with fishing equipment. A Cheerios box top and my personal dime had purchased ten small hooks, three flies, leader, line, a red-and-white bobber, and three thin pieces of bamboo which fit snugly into one pole. Such a deal! Such a shrewd fellow I felt myself to be.

A leader of brothers indeed.

On a bright blue morning we chopped bits of bacon into a pouch, left the tent on high ground, and went forth fishing and to fish. We sought a mountain stream, though we ourselves did not depart the trail down from the campground. Fortunately, that same trail became a wooden bridge which crossed furious roaring waters, the crashing of a falls from the slower bed of a stream.

A mountain stream! There, to our right, before it dived down into the rocky chasm below this bridge, was a mountain stream. Filled with fishes, certainly. We had found it.

But the bridge joined two high walls of stone, and even the slower stream came through a narrow defile.

But I was a shrewd fellow in those days, a leader, like I said. I noticed that a narrow ledge snaked away from the far end of the bridge, that it went beneath the belly of a huge boulder and therefore was hidden from the view of lesser scouts. If we could crawl that ledge on hands and knees through its narrowest part, ducking low for the boulder, why, we'd come to a widening, a hemisphere of stone big enough to sit on, from which to dangle our legs, a sort of fortress of stone since the wall went up from that ledge a flat twelve feet and down again from that ledge another twelve feet. Perfect. Safe from attacks. Good for fishing.

I led my blinking brothers thither. None questioned me. I was the oldest. Besides, I was the one with foresight enough to have purchased a fishing pole.

"You got to flatten out here," I called back, grunting in order to fit beneath the outcropping boulder. They did. One by one they arrived with me in a fine, round hideout. Above the sheer rock some trees leaned over and looked down upon us. Below our feet there turned a lucid pool of water, itself some twelve feet deep.

And so the Brothers Wangerin, Sons of Gladness and Glory, began to spend a fine day fishing.

We took turns with the pole.

The bacon didn't work, but—as a sign of our favor with all the world—the trees dropped down on silken threads some tiny green worms, exactly the size of our tiny hooks. We reached out and plucked worms from the air, baited the hooks, and caught (truly, truly) several fingerling fish. Oh, it was a good day! All that we needed we had.

Then came my father.

We didn't see him at first. We weren't thinking about him, so filled with ourselves were we, our chatting and our various successes.

But I heard through the water's roar a cry.

Distant, distant: *Wally!*

I glanced up and to my right—where the water dropped over stone, where the bridge arched it—and I almost glanced away again, but a wild waving caught my eye.

WALLY! WALLY! WALLY!

"Dad?" Yes!—it was Dad. "Hey, look, you guys. There's Dad leaning over the bridge."

They all looked, and straightway Philip started to cry, and then Mike, too. Paul dropped my pole into the water twelve feet below. And I saw in our father's eyes a terror I had never seen before.

WALLY, HOW DID YOU GET OVER THERE?

Over here? I looked around.

Suddenly *here* was no fortress at all. It was a precipice, a sheer stone drop to a drowning water, and *that* water rushed toward a thundering falls far, far below my father. With his eyes I saw what I had not seen before. In his seeing (which loved us terribly) I saw our peril.

He was crying out as loud as he could: *WALLY, COME HERE! COME HERE!*

But the ledge by which we'd come had shrunk. It was thin as a lip now. The hairs on my neck had started to tingle, and my butt grew roots. I couldn't move. Neither did my brothers. I didn't even shake my head. I was afraid that any motion at all would pitch me headlong into the pool below. I gaped at my father, speechless.

He stopped waving. He lowered his arms and stopped shouting. He stood for an eternal moment looking at us from the bridge, and then his mouth formed the word, *Wait*. We couldn't hear it. He didn't lift his voice. Quietly under the booming waters he whispered, *Wait*.

Then he bent down and removed his shoes. At the near end of the bridge, he bent down farther, farther, until he was on his stomach, worming forward, knocking dust and pebbles by his body into the stream, bowing beneath the enormous boulder that blocked our freedom.

"Dad's coming. See him?"

"Yep, Dad's coming."

"I knew he would."

He pulled himself ahead on the points of his elbows, like the infantry beneath barbed wire, his face drawn and anxious. He was wearing shorts and a long-sleeved flannel shirt. Red with darker red squares. I remember.

When he came into our tiny cove, he turned on his belly and hissed to the youngest of us, "Mike, take my heel." Mike was six. He didn't.

"Mike, *now!*" Dad shouted above the waterfall with real anger. "Grab my heel in your hand and follow me."

You should know that my father is by nature and breeding a formal man. I don't recall that he often appeared in public wearing short-sleeved shirts. Nor would he permit people to call him by his first name, asking rather that they address him according to his position, his title and degree. Even today the most familiar name he will respond to is "Doc." Dad is two-legged and upright. Dad is organized, controlled, clean, precise, dignified, decorous, civil— and formal.

What a descent it was, therefore, and what a sweet humiliation, that he should on his stomach scrabble this way and that, coming on stone then going again, pulling after him one son after the other: Michael, Philip, Paul.

And then me.

"Wally, grab my heel. Follow me."

It wasn't he who had put us in these straits. Nevertheless, he chose to enter them with us, in order to take us out with him. It was foolishness that put us here. It was love that brought him.

So he measured the motion of his long leg by the length of my small arm, and he never pulled farther than I could reach. The waters roared and were troubled; the granite shook with the swelling thereof. But my father was present, and very present. I felt the flesh of his heel in my hand, leading me; and I was still in my soul. I ceased to be afraid.

That stony cove had not been a refuge at all but a danger. Rather, my father in love bore refuge unto me; my father bore me back to safety again. So I did not die in the day of my great stupidity. I lived.

Thus is the kingdom of heaven likened unto a certain man whose eldest son was a nincompoop—

BUT WHEN I
BECAME A MAN

I REMEMBER THE DIFFICULT ritual of my confirmation—when at the age of thirteen I stood in front of the whole church and confirmed my faith in my Lord Jesus.

It felt that it happened wrong for me.

In fact, it happened right; but that feeling of personal terror was a measure of the personal, important, and public step this infant took toward adulthood. Spiritual and communal independence is, when it is real, a scary thing.

My confirmation class consisted of five students. There were two girls, sisters, who commonly pulled my hair on Saturday mornings, protesting in thick accents that they liked me, they *liked* me, then falling absolutely silent when the pastor arrived and the lesson began. They were Dutch immigrants, strong as to muscles, weak as to English. There was one boy who truly did befriend me but who could memorize nothing and who likewise subsided into an unteachable silence when actual class work began. There was a boy who set himself in direct, perpetual competition with me, a glittery-eyed bird of a fellow, a crouching raptor-bird of a fellow. And then there was me—bespectacled, small of stature, grotesque as to hair in which I suffered explosions of cowlick on the back of my head, and as to intellect, passable. I could memorize. Well, and I *had* to memorize, didn't I? In those days my father was the president of Concordia College in Edmonton, Alberta, Canada, a Lutheran, Christian institution. His reputation, therefore, would be affected by my public performance of matters faithful and pious—and that's exactly what was coming: confirmation started with an examination in front of the whole congregation and all my family and God and everybody. Dad is "Walter." I am "Walter." I am his oldest child. I had to uphold the name. I memorized. I memorized everything in the catechism. I memorized *both* the answers *and* the questions *and* the Bible passages that proved those answers to be right.

I ate that book like Ezekiel.

Grim.

I had to.

So on Saturday mornings Pastor Walter Schoepf said to one boy, "What does this mean?" And that boy always said, "Umm. Umm." He didn't know.

So the pastor turned to the two sisters and said, "What does this mean?" Well, but they remained serenely innocent of questions and answers and reputations and English, too. No fears of failure in them. No pressures on their pretty heads.

So then the pastor—all he had to do was say, "Wally." He didn't even have to say again, "What does this mean?" because I memorized questions. Just looked at me and said, "Wally"—and I popped up and recited: "I believe that Jesus Christ, true God, begotten of the Father from—"

All at once (but so regularly that I grew gun-shy in my recitations, waiting for this attack) the competitive fellow, unable to contain himself longer, erupted knowledge, trembling and shouting: "ALSO-TRUE-MAN-BORN-OF-THE-VIRGIN-MARY-IS-MY...."

There was much to wrack my nerves.

So much depends, so much depends, so much depends upon Wally. . . .

The day of confirmation drew near. One week away.

My mother took me downtown to shop. We got me new underwear, new shoes, a shirt, and a new blue suit. Expensive raiment. All this made my heart pound, thinking, thinking: *They're putting money into this thing!* They loved me, of course. They expected me to do well—and to be worthy of a new blue suit.

Would they, then, in the actual event, be proud of me?

On Saturday—our last class, the day before The Day—the Dutch sisters pulled my hair. Routine. But it hurt. And it made me think about my looks for tomorrow. I decided that they pulled my hair because the cowlick invited exactly such scorn. The cowlick, as it were, deserved it.

So that night I took a careful bath, cleaning everything with a scrubbing brush. Toenails. Ears. My whole unbeautiful body. My mortified face. It's too bad I didn't have good looks. But maybe I didn't deserve good looks. *That raptor-bird boy had a certain glittering intensity and dark grooming that made him good-looking.* I thought of my competition, and I thought: *Well, but there is one thing I can do,* and I did—

When I got out of the tub, I didn't dry my hair. I combed it dripping wet. Then I got a nylon stocking from my mother's drawer and rolled it up into a tight hat and put it on my wet, straight hair and rolled it down again over my ears. I wore it to bed. I planned to have perfect hair tomorrow. That's what I could do for my mother and her expectations and her expensive blue suit, for my father and his reputation and our name. At least I could have one perfect thing.

So much depends upon a Wally beautiful with learning—

I lay perfectly still. I prayed a lot that night. Mostly the Lord's Prayer, though, because I kept losing my place in the middle and had to start over and over again. Pastor Schoepf kept coming in and saying, *What does this mean?* Somebody would quote part of the Apostles' Creed, "—And in Jesus Christ, his only Son, our Lord," and then Pastor Schoepf would interrupt and say, *What does this mean?* So I kept losing my place in the Lord's Prayer—which I wasn't saying from memory so much as really trying to pray it.

Well, at that time I was already the oldest of seven sisters and brothers. My confirmation was the first. And Aunt Erna had come all the way from St. Louis because she was my sponsor at my baptism, and she told me that she had a present for me, and she even told me what it was: a King James Bible with onion-skin pages, a very delicate thing; but she also said that she wouldn't give it to me until after my examination, so I better do well in this examination.

So much depends upon...

On the morning of the Sunday of my confirmation I put on my new underwear and my new shirt and my new blue suit. I went into the bathroom. Standing in front of the mirror I rolled up the nylon stocking, careful not to muss a hair on my head. The front looked flat, wispy, obedient, very nice—

But suddenly there shot up from the back of my scalp a whole rooster tail of a cowlick! Oh, no! Oh, *no!* It was like a broom sticking up. It was huge and waving and happy to be there, like it wanted to come to the party, too. I pressed it down with the flat of my hand, and that actually hurt the roots. It just jumped up again. *Oh, no, dear Jesus, no! No!* What would people say about me now?

I took a brush. I flooded it with water. I slicked and slicked my hair until the cowlick grew too heavy to rise again. I was, with great perturbation, drowning a cowlick, killing it. I wanted it dead on the Sunday of my confirmation.

So, then, my father drove me to church, his grim and dripping Ezekiel. I got to sit in front. Mom sat in the back seat. They let me out first.

So, then, I was walking up the path to the church door, my back to the car, wondering whether they were watching me and whether they were proud of me now, whether maybe they were even mentioning out loud to one another that this was their oldest son about to engage in an act of extraordinary courage—when I felt one single cowlick hair pop up: *Ping!* Immediately I reached back and yanked it out and kept on walking.

So, then, all five of us dressed in white robes behind the pastor— the confirmation class—processed up the aisle of the sanctuary while the congregation stood on either side singing a hymn. The church was absolutely jammed with people. I kept my eyes properly forward, but I couldn't sing. There was no spit left in my mouth. I was the shortest confirmand—so how was I to maintain dignity and uphold the family name? A hair popped up. With one hand I covered my mouth to cough; but the cough was a fake to hide what my other hand did; it plucked that hair out of my head.

Finally we sat down upon five chairs that were arranged like a little U in the chancel, our backs to the congregation (but we could hear and we could feel the overwhelming weight of so many people leaning forward to listen and to judge). Pastor Schoepf stood up in front of us rubbing his hands. About to begin. He had the questions on a sheet of paper. We were supposed to have the answers in our heads. A hair popped up on the back of mine and began to wave to the congregation. This time I didn't try to hide the gesture: I pulled it out.

Today as an adult, a father and a pastor too, I declare that my terror in that moment—caught, as it were, between the millstones of responsibility and fear—had its holy purpose. Our present society has few true rites of initiation by which a child can leave childhood and enter, through the valiant accomplishment of a significant task, adulthood with all its rights and responsibilities.

How is he to know that a change has taken place, both in him and in the community's regard for him? How is her very soul to recognize that she must—and can!—shoulder a new role? And how is the community itself to be persuaded to treat the individual differently hereafter? Such a radical shift both in self-awareness and in communal relationships requires an event to mark the change and actually to effect it. It doesn't always happen by unconscious development. In fact, precisely because we *don't* attend as well to such rites of initiation as cultures foreign, primitive, and past, we are a society infested with grown-ups stalled in their childhood, people of age still stuck in immaturity, people unable or unwilling to take responsibility for themselves, people as self-absorbed as children because they are, in spirit if not in body, children.

Their chrysalis never broke nor opened. They never emerged completely whole and capable of high, frightening, independent flight. There never was a rite.

But such ritual must be, as all rituals are, an *event*. And that event must involve a *task* to be accomplished by the initiate. The task, then, must be a personal *experience*, not merely some received piece of information or money or status without the fear and the possible failure of personal action. It must be an experience which relies on the self and God alone, so that the initiate can truly feel the new definitions of her being and the change they represent. Such persuasion comes not so much by words and teaching as by crisis and survival. The task must be *significant*, not some safe parody of adult duties, not a "cute" conferring of honor upon children for no deserving except that we love them. If it is significant—crucial to one's future, so difficult as to threaten failure and, at the same time, to honor success with an honest praise—then passing the test is a genuine entrance into adulthood. Finally, the task must be *public*. The whole society might then honor and admit the change of one individual, receiving noisily a new adult within itself as a responsible citizen.

Confirmation was my initiation.

I can conceive of nothing more significant than that I should, of my own heart and strength and mind, confirm that God is God and is my Lord. This was not some childish entertainment for my congregation. This was in fact a matter of life and death. I knew so by the great burden placed upon me, father and mother and aunt and people. I know it better now for the greater consequence of faith. Life and death: this was no cliché. I would live or die by this divine relationship. Lo, I was crossing into a maturity of faith. In baptism Jesus claimed me. Confirmation, now, completed that holy moment as I independently and with full knowledge claimed him: my Lord.

Terrible, terrible, beautiful! Filled with anxiety before the task, because of the task, because of its monumental importance; trembling, swallowing, standing here at the edge of adulthood, standing here on the precipice 'twixt heaven and hell—

Pastor Schoepf glared at the Dutch girls with a sort of haggard fear. He had already endured three *Umms* and silence from the poor boy who could memorize nothing. The pastor now said to one sister, "What does this mean?"

"*Vass?*" she said, blinking.

He turned to the other sister, "And in Jesus Christ, his only Son, our Lord. It's the second article of the Creed. What does this mean?"

The second sister smiled blithely, showing two stalactites of teeth, monsters of white indifference. The pastor swallowed, glanced at the heavy ocean of folks behind us, and said, "Wally, please, what does this mean?"

I stood up.

That small motion caused a bush of hair to spring up from the back of my head, nodding and grinning at the congregation. I was tempted to tear it out in tufts and handfuls, furious that the one thing which I had hoped would be perfect turned out to betray me. That laughing cowlick! That uninvited idiot! That ugliness—

In the minute while I stood hesitating and Pastor Schoepf's expression grew more and more desperate, my competitive classmate started to answer in a low hiss: "I-believe-that-Jesus-Christ-true—"

And a marvelous thing occurred.

I thought, *I can do this myself,* and straightway, at the top of my lungs, I began to bellow: "NO, NOT YOU, GERALD—*I* BELIEVE THAT JESUS CHRIST, TRUE GOD—"

Such a rush of holy energy blew through me that I *loved* the thing I was saying. I was not reciting. I *meant* it. I meant it with so complete a joy that I forgot about my cowlick.

"—JESUS CHRIST, TRUE GOD, BEGOTTEN OF THE FATHER FROM ETERNITY—"

Oh, I boomed the affirmation. I shouted sweetly oblivious of anyone else's opinion or judgment. I had broken *through!*

"—AND ALSO TRUE MAN, BORN OF THE VIRGIN MARY—"

While I roared forth the words of my own stout heart, I truly forgot about my father and his reputation, my aunt and her gift, the pastor and my classmates and anyone else whom I was supposed to represent except God, except my God. Was my mother proud of me?

O let her be proud forever of this (for by this I rose on my own strong legs and took my stance among the saints), that I turned to the church and shouted with baby abandon:

"THAT JESUS IS MY LORD!"

CRY

NOT LONG AGO I saw a small girl squatting by a rack of coloring books in the narrow aisle of a grocery store. Altogether absorbed, she touched a tiny forefinger to the staring paper eye of Raggedy Ann.

The kid and the picture: each was lost in the eyes of the other, until I approached them pushing a cart whose right front wheel flapped ridiculously. The sound awoke the child, who glanced up toward me.

At first her face was composed with gladness, ready to chat. I think she thought I was her mother coming.

But then her eyes widened. She peered left and right, starting to stand up and murmuring, "Mommy? Mommy?"

There was no one else at all in the aisle.

When she stood, I saw that the hem of the girl's skirt had gotten caught in the band of her underpants. That small lapse and my complete inability to do anything about it (though this mustachioed man is himself a parent and would have unmussed his own daughter easily) caused in me a sharp sense our alienation, one from the other.

I *felt* the panic in the poor child's eyes, the slackening of her lips. Raggedy Ann hit the floor. Gaping at me, the girl gulped air and shrieked at the top of her lungs: "MOMMY! MOMMY, WHERE ARE YOU?"

Little girl abandoned. That fear, when we are suffering it, overwhelms every other consideration. Neatness, social graces, how we are seen or how we *seem*, reputation, physical hunger, nakedness, even, and dangers—these all are diminished by the greater dismay of our personal abandonment, complete alienation. This may be, in fact, the central horror of dying, that we shall be left all alone in the universe.

We all suffer this fear; but children are the quicker to express it. Children are shameless, screaming, *Don't leave me! Come with me!*
I might never find my way home again!

61

Actually, her mother was only an aisle away, right here, but out of sight. At her baby's shrieking she came running, grinning apologies, embarrassed by the outburst and her public association to it. She kept nodding and smiling at me as if I were standing in judgment on her parenting.

The girl, on the other hand, straightway drove her face into her mother's stomach and boo-hooed sobs of immense relief. No, *she* was not embarrassed. She knew and she would pursue her priorities until comfort had come and she was content again.

As for myself, I left the episode still bearing her fear in my bosom. The feeling is altogether too familiar. As a child I suffered terrible bouts of homesickness. I bore the pain of abandonment within me as if it were a bowl filled with water: too swift a motion, too sudden an emotion, and the water would slop out, and I would find myself weeping, helpless to stop the flow of my tears. So I learned to walk with fierce restraint and a perpetual circumspection. I would keep all things balanced within me. I would maintain a sober expression always, whatever befell. I would not cry.

What I learned young, I have practiced for much of my adulthood. I am controlled. I will not be put to shame. If I showed such fear as openly as the child does, why, I would burn with humiliation, compounding the primary terror with this secondary loss of face. Therefore I tuck loneliness behind a measured sobriety, wherever I go.

I am not afraid. I am strong.

I—

While I was a student at Concordia, an all-male boarding school which prepared youth for the Lutheran ministry (while I was, I mean to say, at a middle point between childhood and early adulthood) my mother once drove me back to school at the end of a summer's break.

It was just the two of us alone in the car. For most of the trip she said nothing. Neither did I, sometimes pretending to sleep, most times just staring out the window and suffering the initial twists of homesickness deep in my abdomen.

That same morning Mom had completed laundering my clothes. For much of the morning, in fact, she had helped me finish my packing—and all had been done in a terrible rush, because I had awoken unprepared. *(I did not want to go.)* But Mom wanted to drive both to the school and back again in a single day. She had planned for an early departure—until she saw her son's great unreadiness.

While we worked, then, and while she watched time tick away, my mother had grown more and more angry with me. She stood in slippers at the ironing board in her bedroom, slapping the hot metal to my shirts, pinching her lips, and with a stentorian silence— with the coldness alone—scolding me every time I brought another shirt for ironing.

I was miserable at our departure.

And long before we arrived at school, then, solitude embraced me like ropes around my chest, crushing the talk within me. Homesickness, as I am now convinced, is related to the fear of abandonment, that primal fear, the infant fear perpetual. If I didn't talk to my mother during the car ride to Concordia, it wasn't because I chose not to talk. It was neither pouting or punishment on my part. I did not talk because I *could* not talk. And if I had tried, I would have cried.

But I am strong. . . .

Then, just as we entered the city, my mother spouted forth an unbroken run of language. Intense, frenetic, gazing hard at the streets ahead, she questioned me regarding common things: type-writers, sheets, my courses, church, food, exercise, underwear, when was I coming home again.

We parked in front of my dormitory, and still she talked. We carried my stuff up to the second floor. Classmates also arriving greeted us with a wave or a word, but Mom persisted, oblivious: she'd make my bed for me this once, she'd show me how to arrange my clothes in the closet, she wanted to know if the dining hall published menus in advance.

And then, when all was unpacked, and the car was empty again, and we stood outside the dorm on the sidewalk awaiting the moment of her return, my mother fell silent again.

We stared down at the ground. At our feet. At the black soil on either side of the cement walk, where a green haze of newly sown grass seemed to float above the dirt. Here and there sprouts of sturdy dandelion had taken root and flourished among the baby grasses.

It must have been a full five minutes that we stood staring downward, saying nothing. I couldn't break the silence. What would I say? I didn't know my mother's thoughts. What if I said the wrong thing?

All at once Mom moved. She stepped onto the soft soil and dropped to her knees and began to yank the dandelions out, one by one.

"How *could* they?" she wailed.

Her gestures were choppy with outrage. She crawled forward, her skirt hiking up her calves, and tossed dandelions into an angry pile.

"How could they," she wailed, "let the lawn go to weed like this? Disgraceful!"

Ah, Mother! You suffered the same as I did, no matter your age! You knew too the wretched desolation of abandonment. . . .

It wasn't the weeds, of course, that hectored her so terribly. It was the mess of human existence. It was separation, initiated by our own human moods, perhaps, but experienced like the abandonment of God, which is called Hell.

And what prolongs the separation? What keeps us homesick, yea, though we are standing side by side and thinking the self-same thoughts? Why, pride. And that, too, is a purely human attribute.

Well, no. Let's be absolutely clear: pride is the attribute of the human *adult*. Very few children know such restraints upon the full expression of their feelings.

Sad, the child will cry. Afraid, the child will scream. Abandoned, the little girl shrieks unto high heaven, and any parent in between will hear her, and come, and comfort her. For this, too, is a human attribute: to comfort those we love.

Oh, I wish we had been children, my mother and I, able to cry and to hug and to heal the dying between us.

Or what shall any of us do when we confront the Last Abandonment?

At that extremest of confrontations, surely, and in all the time between then and now, it is no shameful thing to cry. To plead aloud with those beloved:

Please.

It terrifies me when you walk away.

Let us—please—repent and make a home together again.

KINDER- UND
HAUSMÄRCHEN

A Preface to "Kinder- und Hausmärchen"

The following sonnet sequence constitutes a genuine investigation into the shared sufferings of mother and son.

This is the nature of poetry: I did not write this material as a remembrance or a record of some separate activity, mental, emotional or spiritual. In fact, the creative process was ITSELF the investigation of my past—to probe, to understand it, and by poetry's formal principles to give form to experiences which otherwise had been too disturbing for either a shape or a name. At the same time (like crossing the waters stone by stone) I moved from poem to poem into the future, reaching toward a genuine reconciliation of the conflict and the sorrows caused by those past experiences. To name them is to know them; to know them is to gain some power over them, and thereby to creep beyond their control toward healing and the hope of renewal.

And this too is the nature of poetry: it can take the poet by storm. I had not planned these sonnets the way I plan a novel, researching it first, sketching outlines, preparing myself to execute the piece. Rather, the first poem appeared of its own accord and demanded me, my full attention and my following.

In those days, at my publisher's request, I was putting together a manuscript of poems already written, revising some, arranging them all for publication as a book. The second part of this manuscript was entitled "My People" and contained pieces written for and about the members of my families. I intended to include an acrostic sonnet dedicated to my father (see the poem at the end of this preface), and suddenly felt an imbalance. There was no comparable piece dedicated to my mother. One spring morning, therefore, just as Thanne was leaving for work, I told her that I would write Mom's poem that day.

When she came home, Thanne found me gaunt and tearful. The poem to my father is a gentle conceit, more mental than emotion, an affectionate game. I had thought to do something like that for my mother. But by its third line I realized that her poem was refusing to be tame. It would, by God, utter truths that never had been uttered before. It would name a cruelty, and it would cry out that name in anger and grief. And so it did.

And so when Thanne came home she found me frightened by my own feelings. Something had been released to prowl around, roaring without restraint or conclusion. We both recognized, then, that this single poem started a process it could not end. The accusations in it left me sodden with guilt—some of it inappropriate, some of it perfectly appropriate.

I said to Thanne, "I have to write another." Just one more, so I thought then. It behooved me, having given voice to my own experience, now to write myself into my mother's experience with equal candor and force.

On the following day, alone in my study I wrote a second poem. But neither did this one complete the process.

This poem only sought my mother's personal point of view, and only as she was an adult, the woman I'd known since infancy. Sought her point of view, I stress, because it did not wholly find it. Nevertheless, the last two lines presented themselves so suddenly and so spontaneously, that a surface seemed to crack, and I met my mother's anguish face-to-face.

This second poem/stepping stone, then—though mostly intellectual— had become necessary by bearing me forward (and backward) into my mother's formative experiences. By pure imagination I moved into the third poem and its discovery, which was the terrible similarity of our experiences, my mother's and mine. In the boil of that poem, too, an astonishing new kinship sprang up between us—yes, though I was entoiled in the drama altogether alone in my study. It is the nature of poetry truly to reveal what had not been known before, and so the world is altered slightly; and it is the nature of the poetic imagination in truth to dialogue with persons not bodily present. Afterward that truth remains, even though the absent one has yet to learn it—for it has become eminently learnable.

The truth of the kinship established in the third poem now gave me the right to repeat my initial accusation, this time under the dear hope that it might be received and understood. Thus, the fourth poem.

Next, in consequence of the third and the fourth, the fifth poem took me backward to find in our common troublous experiences (to find this for the first time, for the first time in my life to name it and know it) a sacred, abiding goodness in spite of all: that the child had contrived to love his mother in, with, and under the conflicts between us. Or that love itself had found a way even through the maze.

And upon THAT recognition, I had marked a concluding change in me. Through poetry I had evolved enough to make a further declaration of love, even in the midst of a living story still unresolved: the sixth piece was the last, had every right to be the last of this episode, this sequence. Thanne agreed. My hollow anguish had been somewhat filled with a healthier food. A personal hope, if not yet a paired reconciliation.

Altogether, the first draft of this sequence took me about a week to write.

SOME NOTES: This little cycle of poems uses the world of Grimms' collected tales as a contextual metaphor through all six sonnets. There is an old-world German flavor throughout, especially established in the first poem:

—Ungesammelt refers to the subtitle of Jakob and Wilhelm Grimms' book of stories: they were gesammelt, that is, "collected, gathered together." The main title was "Kinder- und Hausmärchen," that is, "Children and Hearth Stories."

—Recchelees is a Middle English word for "reckless, heedless, negligent—careless, lacking care."

—Dodgson is Charles Dodgson, who wrote Alice in Wonderland *under the pen name Lewis Carroll.*

—The Mother Hölle *in poem v also entitles her own tale among the Grimms' collection.* Hässliches *means "hateful."*

—*Poem vi is based on the Grimm tale, "Jorinda and Joringel." In the German version, the unarticulated sound is not "jug," but* "zickut."

Here is the poem written to my father, which triggered the formal outpouring to my mother:

Father, See Me Seeing You

W hen have we seen our changings in a glass?
A rrest me in your mirroring eye, and I will
L oose my habilimental privacy
T ruly to smile at you; smile back at me.
E ncounter my laughter; laugh back . . . remarkable!
R emark it: me, you, is, to be, and was!

W hen has anyone seen new wrinkles screw
A round his face, or watched age grace him, till
N ow? And mere reflected smiles are spectral, thin;
G lassy smiles fade as soon as guilt or sin
E rase the smile progenitor. But MY guilt,
R eflected in MY progenitor—in you—
I s atoned, and lo! One smile remains.
N o, two: but two's one in the glass of our singular names.

Kinder- und Hausmärchen

i.

My mother's tongue was wooden, straight, a broom
Projecting from her mouth, her hair the brambles.
She cleaned house like the north wind, cold, white, grim—
Jakob! Wilhelm! You found her *ungesammelt*
In God knows what thatched *Bauern* cottages:
What did it serve, putting her back together?
Philology? *Recchelees* sciences!

My Mother's tongue was wooden. Write that after
You've written how she licked my skin the way
The medieval bear licked cubs to shape.

My mother's mouth was wooden. Dodgson may
Have met her peppered, yes; but he escaped
To *clepe* her "Duchess." I (my mother's face
Was Teuton) lived the tale as commonplace.

ii.

Blame, so we blame her—but who thinks the tale
Which tells his childhood governed, too, his mother?
What could she choose to do?
    If she were frail
The work would kill her: *Storm, then, through another*
Summer!
    If she were passionate, they'd damn
Her for a gypsy; passion, though, was proper
For rearing proper, upright children: *One*
Became the other.
    If she wept at color,
Words, dusk, the lark, or thought, they'd cluck and sing
Of Bedlam; if she laughed too longingly
Or loose, her uterus was wandering—
So rage found reason in her progeny.

    Peter, Peter! You made that woman wild
    You kept inside the pumpkin of your child.

iii.

I remember your cellar, now. Do you?—
Clean concrete tubs, a glass-ribbed scrubbing board,
And a smell—(Grandma had dry buttocks, bald
Armpits, leather intestines, a mouth that chewed
Blasphemies silently, although the Lord
God still issued commandments she still heard,
Adding them chunk by chunk to the coal pile,
Stirring a Sinaitic dust)—the smell
Grandma wore was the odor in your cel-
Lar, remember? It was the house you grew
Up in. So here's my question: had you, too,
For lies, to bite Fels Naphtha soap, and chew?

Mother, Mother—Gretel! We had one mother
After all. I'm Hansel! I am your brother.

iv.

Yes, there were giants in those days and in
Our world. Yes, they despised you. And Yes, they'd
Kill you if they could. But you couldn't slay
Them, so it was a standoff, stick for sin.

Giants: Sweet Acid Gossip, gross as air;
You smelled your name in breezes like scorched hair;
Outdoors you grew fearful, but indoors you
Grew furious, fumbling for what to do.

Giants: those women all were members of
One body, like a ball of bees, a fist
Of snakes, or Jesus. To assault or to love
Them singly killed no more than cut a mist.

Giants! So you sent me forth, full of rage—
Your rage, though it felt like mine; full of rage—
For them, though it felt like me; full of rage,
Like a knot stick thrust down my throat, a rage

To beat your giants with: *Stick, beat! Stick, beat!*
The stick said, *whom?* But I (a child) said, "Me."

V.

Mother Hölle, do you know how much I loved you?
Under the well and in its meadows—do you know?
It was I who shook down red ripe apples when they begged me,
I who shook your feather ticking, making snow.

Under the well, in sunken meadows, in the cottage
Where you dwelt dreamly, Mother, I obeyed you well.
In the glare light of common day we were another
Pair, *hässliches,* perhaps—but my yearning cast such spells!

I rose from the well wet with gold (all this is true)
And I, flushed with obedience and its reward,
Came home: *"Unser goldener Junge is wieder hie!"*
You rushed to me, you lady longing rich young lords. . . .
Never (I breathed submerged, I breathed through large eyes, through
Wish within that well) *never* did I not love you!

vi.

And now I search the bloodred rose
Whose center cups one pearl (a dew
Drop, beautiful and trembling) whose
Charm is the *Schamir*, to undo

The doors, to set the captives free.
I dreamed you were a nightingale.
Zicküt was all you croaked for me.
A wire cage kept you, and travail—

I dreamed the bloodred rose, its touch
Alone, would spring that cage and hush
Your grief and shift your shape, all three.

The bloodred rose, too, grows encaged.
Bones are its bares—but I will break
My breast to break you, Mother, free.

THE PASTOR OF CHILDREN AND PARENTS TOGETHER

TURN AND BECOME
LIKE LITTLE CHILDREN

GIVE US, O LORD, clean eyes, uncomplicated hearts, and guileless tongues.

Make us like children again!

Here is an irony: when we are still children, we might be the best that we're ever to be—yet we yearn to throw off childhood. We rush to teenagerhood, a worser state in every way, all the while thinking we're getting better.

Let me explain. . . .

When we are children we're likelier to be kinder because we are small in an overwhelming world, and smallness keeps us humble. We identify with them the world considers inferior, helping the helpless and the infirm.

But children wish they weren't children. Smallness is itself a bafflement, a vulnerability. Children rush, therefore, toward the biggerness and the blunt authority of their betters, the teenagers.

Again. . . .

When we are little children we're likelier to be honest. That doesn't mean we're likelier to be *right;* but the honesty alone—our inability to say anything except what we ourselves see of the world—is wondrously effective and refreshing. "But the king has no clothes on!" cries the kid, an observation both honest and right and therefore revolutionary in a kingdom where politics means sucking up and where favors are earned by flattery.

Ah, but that same kid wishes he were older. Soon enough, then, he learns to dissemble, and soon he is buttering his peers, if not his elders—and then he's a teenager surely.

And again. . . .

When we are wide-eyed children the world is filled with things both visible and invisible, things material and immaterial. We make no distinction between the two. There are ghosts. There is also God. These are as real as the walls of our bedrooms and the mouths of our mothers. And that which is real we honor by obeying, by accommodating its presence in our lives and our behaviors. We fear the ghosts. We pray to God.

And we ourselves are spiritual beings too, therefore: small bright bundles of body-and-soul. There is a glory around our heads of which we're unaware but which renders us radiantly lovely since those who see angels do shine as well an ethereal light.

But children are soon ashamed to be children. They're dazzled, rather, by the cold (and self-protective) cynicism of punk teenagers for whom nothing is honorable, by whom nothing need be obeyed (or else one loses one's rep, one's rap, and one's glory). The world of the teen seeks matter and sensation, sound and color and clothes and spasmodic satisfactions—and everything spiritual proves to have been a conspiracy of elders to keep their children on chains.

So we rush to throw off the best we might ever be and to put on instead the dead-slouch, know-it-all, hard-as-steel, lank-lipped sneer of the cynic.

So we are children no longer. This wish is always granted slower than we would and sooner that it should—but this wish is always granted.

Yet, when we were children we laughed without embarrassment. We hooted and giggled and roared till our sides cracked and our cheek muscles ached. The unselfconscious laughter rang very true, like bells in a blue sky, and therefore taught our elders themselves how to laugh again.

When we were children we could gasp with delight at a sudden, beautiful thing, yearning to touch it. We didn't worry whether our notions of beauty were naive. We didn't pretend sophistication. We were not proud; therefore, we could not be humiliated. But our unsullied joy was itself like leadership to all God's creatures, a call to be at peace together.

When we were children our loving was given immediate expression. We *said* it. We *showed* it. We would throw our arms around beloved people and kiss them and purr to be kissed in return. No one had to guess whether we loved. Nor did love seem either a weakness that must be hidden or else a physical desire that must be gratified. Love made us happy. We liked to be happy. And so we were leaders even of whole countries into the image and the command of God—Who *is* Love.

When we were children we accepted forgiveness completely. It truly did—when it was truly given—ease us and allow us to begin again, *anōthen*, as new as one just come down from heaven. We could bounce back from the most grievous sins so quickly that adults wondered whether we had truly repented. Oh, we had repented. Children can move to sorrow instantly and instantly to gladness again, yet feel both moods profoundly. This is the emotional nimbleness of those who have not yet sickened their feelings with self-analysis nor thickened their motives with ambition.

Those who fly swiftly to delight, who fear not to express their love, who believe completely in forgiveness—well, they are fearless. And so it is that the sucking child plays blithely on the hole of the asp, and the weaned one scares her elders by putting her hands on the adder's den.

But then—children don't want to be children.

They want to grow hair in smooth places, immediately to cut it off again.

They want to smear outrageous colors on places God had painted pink and to punch holes in places God had made smooth. This is called "style."

They pretend to love the things they don't and feign indifference for things they love unspeakably. This is called "fashion."

Because their peers do, they walk in streets instead of on sidewalks; they wear jeans beaten old before the purchase; they do not lace their tennis shoes; they congregate on corners like lemmings going nowhere, doing nothing. This is called "doing my own thing."

They laugh when it isn't funny and do not laugh when it is. This is called "cool."

When they don't feel something, they act as if they do, and they exaggerate the act for fear that someone may notice it's only an act. They fear to be different from peers. When, however, they feel an emotion deeply (whether rejoicing or love or repentance) they mask the mood and gaze wanly into the distance.

They are not what they are; and what they are they strive to hide. This is called "teenager." It is considered an advance over childhood. It's the rush from innocence into society. It's a determined dispersal of the clouds of glory which we trailed when first we came from God.

It is a pity.

"Give us clean eyes, uncomplicated hearts, and guileless tongues, O Lord!"

That, immediately, was my prayer when I found among my letters the following, unselfconscious "summery" by Erica Ulrey. Her grandmother had read to the child a book of mine. The book was about Jesus. Then Erica took pen and printed on paper and mailed to me these words:

SUMMERY JESUS STORY

Well it all started out when an angle came to mary and told her that she was going to have a baby, it would be a boy, a boy name jesu. He would be the son of the Lord. They traveled to drusilem. They knocked on inkerp's door but know one had room. So they went to a stable. She had the baby.

Jesus grew older when he was 20 or 30. He went and told stories. He got bapties because he wanted to have sins. He told Peater that his enimes would kill him. Jesus arived in drusilem on a donkey. Children were waving palm limes. Jesus went in two the Temple and open the cages of animals tiping taples. His enimes came and hung him up on a cross. After three day's his desiples came to his grave, and angle stood in front of his grave. He was not in the grave. They found Jesus. They thought he was a gost but he had the holes in his hands. Then one day Jesus said I will be up in hevan. The End.

O sisters and brothers (so often so teenish in spite of our years, because we desire the approval of peers) if we would turn and become like little Erica, then such fearless and faithful contemplations of the gravest mysteries need never end for us as well.

No, not ever: for it is as little children that we shall enter the kingdom of heaven.

I LOVE THEE, BABY B

BRANDON MICHAEL PIPER. What a sober name for a two-year-old! It sounds senatorial. It seems an executive's name.

But you bear the big name well, my little godson. You've a stalwart constitution and a sweetness of spirit that softens me when I hold you. No, the name is not too large; rather, you make the name foursquare and strong.

Dear Brandon:

Perhaps you won't remember in the years to come (but I will always remember) that I am the one who holds you these Sunday mornings during Bible class. Your mother and your father both have duties; but I have two arms free and a large heart, and I am your godfather, and I love you.

You cling to me, child. Stump-arms soft on pliable bone, you grip my neck. You lock your legs around my body. I couch your butt on my forearm and press you to my chest and feel the deep warmth of your trusting infancy. Oh, Brandon! You hallow me with such trust! You make me noble and kind.

They call you "B," don't they? "Baby B." A lighter, lesser name than the one you'll carry into adulthood but one conferred by affections. I remember when I was trying to distract you in Bible class and happened to draw that letter. You read it. You astonished me by the recognition. "Beeeee," you murmured with wonder, gazing at yourself. Then, "Ef," you said when I made an *F*. And "Ay" and "Eeeee."

This kid's a prodigy, reading at two! This kid is my godson.

Perhaps in the years to come you will also forget that your baby bones were not always stalwart or so strong. You limped. No complaint. You seemed to take this particular development for granted. But you began to favor one leg over the other, and walking became a difficulty.

In fact, it was on a Sunday morning that I first became aware of trouble. Your leg came too close to my coffee cup; I shifted it, and you whispered, "Ow," so fleetingly—but then without a sound you started to cry. You gazed at me with a sort of pleading through the tears that shined in your Brandon eyes, and I saw again that astonishing trust. You trusted your godfather somehow to help. Oh, Baby B, how could I? I didn't know what hurt you. Too deep. The trouble was hidden too deeply in your tiny body.

But your parents were ahead of me. They had already planned to take you to the doctor.

And this is a thing I hope you will forget completely: the X-rays revealed a growth high in your leg, near the hip, against the thighbone.

Your mother and father listened as the doctor enumerated the possible problems, from a cyst to a malignancy. Then he explained which procedures he would advise. But his language was indirect and faintly patronizing. He described "windows" into your leg—until your mother fixed him with a baleful eye and said, "If you don't want a hysterical mother here, you'd better speak clearly to me." The doctor blinked and began in a more respectful tone to use the word "biopsy."

You have bold parents, B. They are patient and faithful. Their patience may—as with silly physicians and sillier children—come sometimes to an end. But never their faith.

They said to the doctor, "Yes, schedule a biopsy. Schedule a biopsy. But we, in the meantime—we will pray for our son."

We all prayed for you, then, Brandon Michael Piper. You won't remember. But the aunts and the uncles, your parents and grandparents and godparents and the whole congregation of Grace commended to heaven both your big name and your little leg.

Someone worried about the intensity of your parents' praying. He said, "But what if the boy's too sick? What if he doesn't get well? Doesn't it scare you that you might lose your faith if God doesn't answer the prayer?"

But your parents said, "We will pray for our son."

You see, Brandon, this was their faith: not that they felt God had to heal you on account of prayer, but rather that they wanted never to stand apart from God, especially not now. Yes, they were scared for you. But they were never, never scared of God, nor ever scared to lose God. They took their Baby B to the steadfast arms of the Father so that *whatever* happened, the love of God would hold it. Might there be a healing? Then give glory to God. Must there be a worse hurt? Then let the dear Lord strengthen everyone when strength would be most needed.

Their prayer was meant neither as a demand nor as magic, neither an ultimatum nor manipulation of the Deity. It was love. It was their highest expression of faith—not faith in your healing, Brandon (though they yearned that) but faith in God.

This is an important distinction which, in the future, you must remember. Your parents' faith did not depend upon God's "correct" answer to their prayer. Instead, the reality of their prayer depended upon their faith. With prayer they encircled you as tightly as you do hug my neck on Sunday mornings—and behold: that circle of faith was the arm of the Almighty.

And then there came the night when you could not sleep because of the pain. You cried, not silently this time. You broke your mama's heart. So that was when the patience of your parents (but not their faith!) came to an end. They bundled you to the hospital, and the biopsy which had been scheduled too many weeks in the future was immediately rescheduled.

Dear Brandon, whatever else you forget in the future, remember this: God loves you.

I was there, my godson, when they signed the love of God upon you—as if God himself wrote his name across your forehead, saying *I own this one; this one is mine.* I was there when they gave you *your* sober, senatorial name, and it became the name of you forever. I was there when they washed you thrice with a purging water, and

I with my own ears heard them say, "Brandon Michael Piper, I baptize you in the name of the Father, and of the Son, and of the Holy Spirit." That's how I became your godfather. That's how the mighty God became your own most holy Father, your final Father after all. That's how the magnificent name of *Brandon Michael* got written into the Book of Life. And that, child, was a healing for any hurt which you shall ever encounter, because it has overcome death itself.

Of course your parents would not lose faith if you weren't healed of this particular problem in your thighbone. They might be very sad for you, but they would not despair—because your baptism had already declared the rising of all your bones in the end.

Whatever else you do in the future, Brandon, hold to the God that now holds you. Pray always as your parents prayed for you. Cling to the body of Jesus more tightly than you do to mine on Sunday mornings. And the God who signed you will love you infinitely, finer, and longer than ever I could—

As it happened, the biopsy proved the growth benign. It shall be removed, together with all memory of a falling limp and the nighttime pain.

And I will continue, Brandon Michael Piper, a little longer to let you sleep on my shoulder in church. But you will grow. You'll pull back from such dependencies upon earthly fathers, godfathers first, flesh fathers second. Even then I will pray for you, my godson, my Baby B.

And this shall be my prayer: that you never pull back from the God who, since your baptism, is your Father forever.

AN INSTRUCTION: THE DIFFERENCE BETWEEN PUNISHMENT AND DISCIPLINE

SHOULD THE PARENT PUNISH or discipline the child?

Prisons punish. By most accounts, that's all they can do. Some parents punish too, but that's not all *we* can do, nor is it what we're charged by God to do. Nor is it healthy.

Rather, it was for discipline that we were set above the children and the children under us.

Punishment administers pain for pain and hurt for hurt. If it is meted in an ethical manner, it makes the pain the criminal gets equal the pain he gave. It balances the social books of right-eousness. And if it loves anything, it loves the law. Or vengeance. Or, at its best, society as a whole. But it does not love the criminal. Simply, he is made to pay *post factum* the debt his crime incurred; and the social order is, by an eye and an eye, a tooth and a tooth, preserved. Society receives the benefit. Except that he will be restrained hereafter, the criminal is scarcely affected or changed: correctional facilities do precious little correcting.

On a level more rude, punishment is merely the expression of someone's discontent, irritation, anger—and then nothing is loved so much as that one's thwarted desires and his own power to say so. Again, nothing changes.

But discipline loves the criminal.

And though discipline also gives pain, unlike punishment it seeks to change the child at the core of his being.

Note, please: the benefit of punishment is for the person or the system administering punishment; but the benefit of discipline is for the one who is *being* disciplined. It is, says the writer to the Hebrews, "for his good, that he may share in holiness." A supernatural benefit!

Moreover, it is a gift of the discipliner to the disciplined, both of whom will suffer the pain of the process: "For the moment all discipline seems painful rather than pleasant; later it yields the peaceful fruit of righteousness to those who have been trained by it." But if a parent says that the pain is "for your own good, you little————," and punishes to relieve himself—for anger's sake or for vengeance or because he's lost control, but in no wise to plant in his child *the peaceful fruit of righteousness*—he lies in his teeth, committing a double treachery and multiple sins in a single swat.

Does the parent seek tears? It is punishment. Does the parent grow frustrated when there are no tears? When there is no sign of pain? It is punishment.

And punishment is not the charge God gave the parents.

Another difference: discipline is an extended and carefully managed event, not a sudden, spontaneous, personal reaction to the child's behavior.

I sat with a mother in her kitchen, visiting. Her daughter toddled in, whining, and yanked the woman's skirt.

"Don't. We're talking," said her mother. She gave the kid a cookie and continued to talk.

But the cookie lasted only a little while. When it was eaten, the child was back, whining again and yanking her mother's skirt.

"I said don't!" She nudged the kid and kept talking.

A third yank earned a vague wave of the hand.

The fourth yank earned a swat on the butt.

And when the child began truly to cry, the mother in exasperation stood up, hoisted the girl, and hauled her from the room. "When will she ever learn?" she said. She punished the kid by dumping her in her crib and closing the bedroom door.

"Punished," I say, because this was in no way a careful event for the child's sake, in love with the child. It was altogether for the parent's desire, peace, and ease.

An event . . .

Let Jesus teach us.

Even as he disciplined Simon Peter, so may we discipline our children—seeking, as he did Peter's, the children's righteousness that they might share in holiness.

The end of such a process is that they know the love of God and their place within it.

It has three steps and a peaceful response to the child's sin. She is of our flesh and we are sinners. She is not different from us. Therefore—

1. Anticipate the sin

Right clearly and with sufficient sadness to indicate the wrong, Jesus said, "You will deny me, even before the rooster crows the morning in." He didn't argue it. He said it. He prepared Peter to recognize the sin when it would occur—for he couldn't change Peter's soul if the sin had never surfaced, nor could he change Peter's mind if the disciple didn't see and acknowledge the sin when it did.

It must be the same for the parents. Choose a few significant rules to be kept in your household (not countless numbers, stirred up by your own continual frustration in the face of having kids around). Choose rules that touch upon the child's deepest righteousness. Consider the two most elemental commandments: loving God, loving others. Let your rules define *this* behavior in the child.

Declare them clearly. Post them if necessary so that the child surely is aware of them. There is no need to argue them. They are not here to restrain the child right now (for our own peace) but for training her when she breaks the rule.

She will break the rule.

That, in fact, is the point. It's her nature. It's the "Adam," the "Eve" you seek to change by discipline. If you anticipate the transgression as much in your emotions (peacefully), as in your planning (this is just step 1), you won't explode at the sin ("You rotten kid! Oh, where did I go wrong?"). Rather, you will be glad that her sinful nature surfaced and gave you the opportunity to teach and revise it. Also, you won't act in anger (punishment) but will in cool love discharge the duty God gave you as a parent.

2. In the very instant of the sin, shine a light on it

Call it wrong and painful to others and self-destructive.

Peter did, of course, deny the Lord exactly as the Lord had said, exactly as the Lord expected. In that instant two things happened: the cock crowed to remind Peter of Jesus' prediction, to apply the name of the sin which Jesus had given it earlier, to persuade Peter that Jesus was, in fact, superior. Peter could not *not* see himself as Jesus had seen him now. He had not kept his promise: "If I must die with you, I will not deny you." Jesus was right (so Peter knows by the predicted rooster crow) and Peter was wrong.

Moreover, in the moment of his denial, Jesus "turned and looked at him." The sin was not antiseptic. It was very personal. It hurt someone whom Peter loved. And Peter must see that in Jesus' wounded eyes. This is *shining a light* on the sin. This is, in the same gesture, shining a light on the sinner. Peter saw himself more clearly now than he had when he boasted.

He went out and wept bitterly.

The pain he caused in someone else is the pain he felt in himself (this is what guilt—a good thing!—accomplishes), so for Peter sin was no longer an abstract concept, but an act both real and dangerous and his own. His personal pain communicates better than any argument, any rational discourse. Such awareness comes in experience.

Let it be the same for the parents. When your child breaks the rule, immediately communicate the wrongness of the act and its painful consequences and the child's responsibility for it. In terms she can understand, define it for her. Speak to both her mind and her soul that she and you—the both of you—have been wounded.

In a special place of the house (rooms define our actions) by a repeated and recognized ritual (for she shall not sin once, but often) name the rule again and mark the details of her breaking it (as Jesus used the rooster to remind Peter of what he'd said in the past). *Do you remember, child? This is the rule. And this is what you did. Do you remember both, child?* So and so: the sin as a sin becomes real unto her in the conversation of your relationship.

Do none of this in anger. Be sad. You love her. You can survive as you are, but she must change for her survival. You have been hurt. Now the hurt must communicate itself to her. For finally it is not your hurt but the child's of which she must be persuaded. Therefore, (ah, me!) let pain define both the general effect of sin and the kid's responsibility—and the ultimate personal suffering of that effect (for destruction circles back, in the end, upon the destroyer). What she feels will speak to her more than rational discourse: you may (though many may not) choose a careful spanking.

"Careful." Act *after* you've named the sin and reminded the child of its consequence—not immediately or passionately.

"Careful." Adhere to the consequence prescribed for any infraction. If it's two weeks' grounding, keep to two weeks, no more, no less. If it's five swats, then let it be five swats, no more for anger, no less for tenderness.

"Careful." Any spanking must hurt the parent equally to the child. A flat hand on a covered butt. Flesh absolutely must feel flesh. I mean that no instrument can come between to increase one's pain and decrease the other's. And there can be no true wound. It is the tactile communication the parent seeks, not punishment. Not punishment. No, not punishment.

And this parent will recognize her love in her own pain. If there is no parental pain, there must be no such discipline. Choose something else!

3. Heal the hurt
This must follow or else what you have done is merely punishment. Please read John 21:15–19.

After the sin Jesus took time and patience to repair the relationship between himself and Peter. More than that, he called Peter to greater faithfulness and mightier action, proving his trust both in the strength of his (Jesus') forgiveness to change the man and in the reality of his (Peter's) change. Thrice Peter had denied the Lord; thrice, therefore, did the Lord ask him to declare his love (and by the third declaration Peter clearly saw the effect of his sin, because he was grieved—reminded and grieved); and thrice Jesus showed confidence in Peter's ministry thereafter, in Peter's worth, in Peter: "Feed my lambs. Tend my sheep. Feed my sheep." *All is well*, the Lord Jesus said by repeating then the words with which he had called Peter in the first place: "Follow me."

All is well.

Once again let it be the same for the parents. There are three necessary gestures at this point, all modeled upon Jesus' gentle ministrations.

When the child's tears subside, speak again the sin in such a way that your love is proven unchanged; speak again the rule that had been broken; speak again the child's personal responsibility in breaking it—but cast your entire talk in the gentlest of terms: love, love—"Do you love me?" Jesus asked in order to give Peter opportunity to prove that he no longer denies but loves.

The sin is not hidden now or else forgotten; you do want the child to change, to move beyond this iniquity, and so you both must from a new vantage confront it. But love outlives the sin and its consequence.

Next, touch the child. Physically. As physically you communicated her wrong, communicate your love. Touch her now not for pain but for gentleness and in soft caress. The touch communicates. Hold her. Hug her. This is critical for finally changing her. Tell her her worth and your abiding, unchanging affection.

Finally, affirm her worth (and prove your renewed trust in her) by giving her specific responsibilities in the household, as Jesus right easily called Peter back into discipleship: *Feed my sheep*. Make the responsibility real, something which, if she does it well, benefits others—benefits *you!*

If you punish only, the spanking shall have satisfied you and there you cease—abusing your kid. If you discipline, this loving satisfies her need for spiritual growth, for it announces her share in holiness, her newness, and your trust.

Now, love is not flaccid.

Parents are not appointed to be the buddies of their children, seeking their affections and praise, seeking ever and ever to keep the kid happy. Parents, rather, are called to be instruments of God for the children, seeking their holiness.

Love does not neglect to discipline. That's negligence. But neither is love the plain demand for obedience by pain. That's punishment.

If we love our children as the Father loves us, that is parenting indeed.

AN INSTRUCTION: INTRODUCING CHILDREN TO THE FAITH

WE CALLED IT CONFIRMATION CLASS when I was young. (See chapter 7 above.) In the Lutheran Church we call it Confirmation Class still, now that I am old and have myself spent years and years as the Pastor who taught it. Other churches have other means for introducing children and youth to the teachings and the commitments of the Faith: Sunday school, youth groups, Pastor's classes, Baptismal Instructions. But all churches acknowledge the responsibility somehow to communicate our most important Christian truths to the next generations, the sons and daughters of our mothers and fathers. And the question becomes: how do we do it? Do we do it well?

Age to age—generation to generation, in fact—our educational methods have changed. Have we lost effectiveness in the change? Or found a method more effective? Or exchanged one strength for another, different strength? One weakness for another?

Under the methods of the previous generation, I learned sternly. All was conducted with a solemn lawfulness (for these matters *were* grave, weren't they?—consisting of life and death.) So: I conned by heart the meaning of the Lord's Prayer, the meaning of the Apostles' Creed, the Commandments and the Sacraments and the Christian Table of Duties—conned, I mean, word for word Martin Luther's explanation of all these things. There was little joy in the exercise; there was, rather, great anxiety to . . . Get. It. *Right!*

PASTOR: "The Fifth Commandment."

WALLY: "Thou shalt not kill."

PASTOR: "What does this mean?"

WALLY: (Standing erect, his thumbs upon his pant-seams) "We should fear and love God that we may not hurt nor harm our neighbor in his body, but help and befriend him in every bodily need."

Therewith, we memorized biblical proof passages to support these meanings. I have these things by heart even still today. Indeed, there *was* value in the severity of my training. But a faith without joy is a faith that knows *about* the Savior, but never yet has *met* him or felt his steadfast gaze upon its face.

During the years of my ministry, on the other hand, new methods of education have risen up to ease us all. And joy might now find voice in the instruction—especially since severity is less and less commended in any "extra-curricular" training which depends upon the youth's own willingness to come and learn at all. This generation must not feel (as, cruelly, I did feel) burdened. Therefore, the giddier spirit and the contentments of the youth themselves have shaped the atmosphere of their religious schoolrooms.

And therefore it is with some dismay that I've watched how this tendency to Good Will has replaced the genuine gravity of these matters (which *do*,—don't they?—train the student in the difference between life and death). No longer need they know the Bible with close familiarity; no longer memorize great portions of Holy Scripture, that the words be handy in circumstances yet to come; no longer need they give a good verbal account for the basic, most important tenets of their Faith and Salvation.

Instead, after classes which have spent more time in personal discussion than in significant instruction, entertaining every thought as equally valuable to any other, requiring teachers to devolve into mere facilitators and thereby allowing the students to lead and to shape the substance of the material—after, I say, even energetic and satisfying discussions, comes something like a public examination. And for this spiritual Rite of Passage the students are asked to prepare themselves. Not, mind you, to gird themselves with the accumulated insights and wisdom of the elder generations; but rather to sit down and write, each student, his and her own statement of faith; in her own words; according to his own lights. And *these* statements, then, are offered to the congregation as proofs of . . . of what, really? Not of the youths' advancement beyond themselves and their own callow experience; proofs, rather, of juvenile sincerity as evidenced by a thirteen-year-old's concept of the Deity: how God Almighty and the Lord Jesus Christ—the Judge and Savior of the world—seem when seen through the eyes of teenagers.

But in many Christian traditions, this instruction accompanies the most transfiguring decision a boy or a girl can make: to accept Jesus, to be baptized into his name, to drown the old and to rise anew. Such instructions are the plans for an entire life to come. And baptism is reserved until a child has attained the age of reason precisely *because* a personal understanding of one's choice and of its consequences is considered essential for a true and faithful participation in the act.

In my tradition, too, confirmation is connected to Baptism. And though, in earth-terms, time has elapsed between the act of Baptism and the instruction of the Baptized, in God's time the two events are one: God initiates the sacramental act, and the child finishes it. God acts in Baptism to establish a relationship with the child, and then the child (having attained the age of understanding) of his own will acts to say "Yes!" to the relationship.

In the waters of Baptism, God says, "You are my child!"

Which word the youth personally confirms by answering, "And you are my Lord!"

In all Christian traditions, then, Baptism elevates the purpose and the practice of the training of our youth in the faith. It should never, therefore, be diluted or diminished, never dismissed as of lesser importance than, say, the glad contentment of our teenagers. Likewise, it should never fall upon the youth as a grim and heavy imposition, crushing the love, suffocating the joy in an entire generation—and thereby diminishing the Church itself.

I think there is a middle way. A third way, actually, as old as story and as new as the weekend movie. I commend it to pastors and teachers, to anyone responsible for passing our culture and our covenant to the next generation.

Some History

My own first year in the parish, during which I undertook the Confirmation Class, was a dismal experience. This was a small congregation in the inner city; and though adults had strong hearts for the faith, their children were altogether undisciplined in religious ritual. I could count on no one's regular attendance. Homework simply did not occur. I could make friends with the kids—and did. But I could not of my own authority persuade them that the topic I taught mattered more than basketball or (in those days) Run-DMC or Nintendo.

By the end of the teaching year, I took the hard line, seeking to establish with *everyone* how seriously we must take this learning, and no one was confirmed. I invited them all back for a second year.

During that year two events happened to shape my confirmation classes ever thereafter.

The first was formed of my Pastoral desperation. I decided to teach each student in his or her own home, under the required attentions of the adult who was raising that child. *I* would go to *them*. And I would make the parent/grandparent/older sibling as much my student as the kid, establishing relationships with both and expecting the older to oversee the younger's personal homework.

But in order to set up *that* labor-intensive program, I first went to each home seeking promises! I wanted a contract in hand by which to encourage (or enforce) the commitment when kids or parents lagged in interest or energy.

So I sat with the whole family. According to my plan, we *all* spoke of our individual readiness to embark on confirmation classes. The atmosphere was completely democratic: if any one of the three of us (child, pastor, guardian) felt unready or unable—or if a parent truly thought the child unready—that single veto moved the question of confirmation on to the next year. But if we all three said "Yes!"— why, I had both the promise and individual good will to go.

The fact that I ended up with five students made possible the regular home visitations. But everyone will recognize how inefficient such a scheme must be. I did not in the following year repeat that part of the performance.

On the other hand, I had learned how crucial is this common covenant. And it would *not* be a covenant if it lacked true choice.

It was the seeking and the saving of the three-way covenant that I continued ever thereafter.

The second event happened Easter Sunday morning that year . . .

I'd come to the church in the wee, dark hours of the morning, in order to pace up and down the central aisle, conning my sermon by heart. This was my Sunday habit: preparation for preaching was as much emotional and spiritual as it was intellectual.

After the sun had arisen, about an hour and a half before worship was to begin, children started to arrive. Without their parents. And since our building had only two large rooms (the fellowship hall below and the sanctuary above) the kids chased through them both, heedless. No parents; no Sunday school teachers either. No adult besides myself! I couldn't think. The sermon dying inside me. I was veering toward panic and schemes of bloody assaults. Where were the teachers? Why were these kids here *now*?

I did not know that the children were not here for Sunday school at all. I did not know that the teachers were *not* here because there was no Sunday school planned. I did not know (no one had told me) that the refrigerator downstairs was filled with cartons of colored eggs. Of *course* the kids were antsy: they were looking for a good time and gifts.

All shot out of patience for the want of a sermon, I shouted to the children, "Sit down!"

They froze mid-run and looked at me. *Sit? Why?*

"Sit down," I said, and the next thing popped unbidden out my mouth: "And I'll tell you a story!"

I'll tell you a story. It was the most natural thing for me to say. And it had its natural effect: the kids sat. All ages sat down in the pews, facing me, filled with anticipation, *ready* for a story. (Well, the inner-city does tend more toward oral communication than to written.)

And because no other story was so immediately to hand than this one, I began by saying, "Jesus was eating supper with his disciples, and he was soooo sad."

The littlest faces fell straightway into lines of deep sorrow. They knew sadness, and with my next words, they *felt* sadness: "Because one of his disciples, one of his friends, was going to go out and rat on him. . . ."

For the next forty minutes I told them the story of Jesus' suffering. I watched them closely. I said that the hero was going to die. They did not believe me! Heroes never die! And they were identifying tightly with this hero. They *liked* Jesus.

When, therefore, I described in detail his arms and hands being nailed to a cross-piece of wood; described in detail how they lifted the cross-piece and Jesus' body up to a stout pole and dropped the whole onto a peg there; when I raised my arms to show the great weight that pulled on them, closing Jesus' chest, causing his own body to suffocate his lungs—why, some ten pairs of children's arms were unconsciously up in the air, same as mine. And faces filled with an unspeakable sorrow. Because I said, "He died. He died. Jesus really did die . . ."

A marvelous thing was occurring in that little sanctuary: by story, twenty-five children had been transported straight back to Jerusalem and to Golgatha.

And then the adults started arriving at church, chirping welcomes back and forth, bringing with them a daffodil morning, and smiting the eyes with their bright Easter finery. The adults entered the sanctuary . . . and found their children all gloomy in the pews. Well, he died! No, there was no joy in the hearts of the children at that moment.

Shuffling mostly, the children moved to sit with their families. They did not sing "Jesus Christ Is Risen Today."

And I was very clear about my sermon now. There was no choice. How could I *not*, for my children's peace of mind, finish the story?

"But that's not all," I said directly to the children. And then I said, "Mary Magdalene was crying. . . ."

I spoke of the early Easter events through Mary's eyes. But when that moment comes when Jesus addresses her by name, I looked straight at Larry Thomas and I said, "Jesus said, 'Larry!' And Jesus said, 'Dee Dee,' 'Charlotte,' 'David.'"

And I saw then, and I testify now to, their genuine wonder and transfiguration. Those who had truly experienced the death of their hero now truly rejoiced in his resurrection. It was no self-manufactured emotion; it was the genuine thing! And it was not in response to the holiday, no; it was in response to the living Lord Jesus Christ.

Out of my weakness and the mistakes of the day emerged this simple (and at the same time ancient) conviction: that story-telling conveys the realities and the relationships of our faith better than almost any other form of communication we have, for in story the child does more than think and analyze and solve and remember; the child actually *experiences* God through Jesus and through Jesus' ministry. The whole of the child is involved in the faith.

Out of these insights the following program was formed.

1. Covenant
This first step into the confirmation class is essentially the same as I have described above, with a few refinements.

—I encourage the teacher/pastor to meet with the candidate and her family in their own homes, not in a large group at the church. These matters must actually *be* personal from the beginning: eyes looking into eyes, the prayers of the pastor embracing the child by name.

—Yes, begin with prayer. Conduct the meeting with formality. This is not a time for cookies or adult laughter and conversation; nor should the child feel in any way patronized. On *her* account is this gathering gently serious. I encourage, if possible, the presence of her Baptismal sponsors as well, especially to establish the relationship between her Baptism and what is about to be.

—Meet *twice* with the candidate and her family, expecting everyone to be at both meetings, since each will be of equal importance. During the first meeting simply discuss confirmation, its meaning in the candidate's life, its practice, what it requires. All this will be under the question: "Are we ready, the three of us, to begin confirmation this year?" But that question is not to be answered at the first meeting. It is too important for swift responses (even if the parents have already discussed it). The space of time between this meeting and the next will surely persuade everyone of the gravity of the class, and make the covenant more felt and thereby more binding.

At the second meeting, after prayer, the pastor/teacher receives the answer. Honor the "no." Open pathways to the repeat of this discussion next year. And for the "yes," have cookies. *Then* a celebration is in order.

—Sometime early, the child should be invited to pick her own confirmation-sponsor from among members of the congregation, for a continual interaction throughout the next two years.

2. The First Year: Meet God
Yes. Two years, not one. But, by making each year its own good experience, the students do not count this a woeful waste of time.

And this is how that first year is spent: by telling the stories. By weaving them, week after week, together, and *thereby* telling the whole story of faith after all.

Listen: religions have and do exist without doctrines and theologies; but no religion has ever existed without a story at its core, not as an *illustration* of some doctrine, but rather as the very truth, the evidence and the testimony of God's action for the sake of the believers.

But a story that goes untold lacks life. It becomes a puzzle to be solved by intellectual analysis alone. And a religion whose story is untold, likewise, lacks life!

For if we never have, by means of the sacred story (the Gospel!) *experienced* the presence, love, activity of our Christ, then we will fall back upon lesser experience; we will fulfill our natural need of religious experience with mere sentimentalities and silly diminishments of God. And so our religion, too, will be diminished.

On the other hand, if all we have of God is our own religion's doctrines, well, then we will begin to worship the most subtle idol of all: our own words *about* Jesus, as if they were the Christ, the Word of God! Such a blindness will never recognize that it *is* blind.

When I was a child, we went Satur-daily to the YMCA where, for a dime, we watched two films. One was a full-length feature (Ma and Pa Kettle; Abbot and Costello), and the other, often a cowboy movie, was a cliff-hanger. We had to come back the next week to see how the Lone Ranger got out of his desperate fix.

When I taught confirmation's first year, I did essentially the same thing, with essentially the same results.

From September to mid-December, while the students sat before me in the pews of the sanctuary, I told key stories of the Old Testament. Each new week I quizzed them on the events of last week's story—both as a test and as the summary that would carry us into this week's episode. I promise you: it is astonishing how much of what is experienced is retained, as opposed to what must be seized and held by intellect alone.

I used "Covenant" as the theme for that half the year: God's first covenant with humanity, in the stories of the creation and the fall; God's second covenant with humanity through Noah; God's third covenant with a single individual, Abraham, then Isaac, then Jacob; God's covenant with a single people at Sinai, after leading them out of Egypt; God's renewal of covenants with Joshua; God's peculiar covenant with King David and his heirs;

and the cries of the prophets against those who break covenant with God.

This theme granted me an unbroken thread through the Old Testament by which to choose the most important stories *and* still to keep them (cliff-hanger-like) in the sequence of a single story which finally must lead to the dramatic new and concluding covenant in the Lord Jesus Christ.

So the stories moved naturally (and carried the confirmation class easily) to the events which the whole congregation was to celebrate in the rest of the year: I told the birth stories through Christmas. I told the stories about *who* Jesus, the Hero, is—and what his ministry looked like—during the weeks after Christmas up to Ash Wednesday. Between Ash Wednesday and Palm Sunday I showed Jesus fighting against all that would kill us: the devil and sin and death. (You see how powerful by *any* standards this story of ours is? Evil things want to kill us.) We walked, those days, through darkness, and hatreds were real, and fears found form and a name.

But then, just as I learned one early Easter Sunday, all things came to a climax at the cross—after which I told of Jesus' resurrection appearances and his entrance into Heaven.

When I speak of this program to other pastors and teachers, they often object: "But we can't tell stories. There's a special skill to telling stories."

I reply that they are right: there *is* a special skill to the craft. But it is both learnable and findable by nearly everyone who can speak in front of children to teach them.

In this case, method follows motive. *How* you tell stories will depend upon *why* you tell stories, and if your personal reasons are right, you will surely tell stories effectively.

There are two rules.

(1) If the story that you are telling is of profound importance unto you—unto *you;* if the tale communicates that without which you could not live, that which seizes your whole heart and mind, then you will find the method and manner by which you personally communicate most important things.

My father-in-law, Martin Bohlmann, was a farmer, not an orator. He listened in church and scarcely spoke. He was the father of four-teen and the grandfather of that village that raises children. When *he* had something to say which he considered of first importance, he would lean slightly forward in his chair, would lower his voice and look folks directly in their eyes; and folks (dozens and dozens of folks) would fall quiet to hear him.

It shall be the same way with you: if it is of the Lord God that you are speaking; and if you love the Lord your God with all your heart with all the strength with all your mind, well, your delivery with have authority and power, though your method be different from every one else's method.

(2) And the second rule is like unto the first. If you do truly love your neighbor; if you love the children unto whom you speak; if you love *them* particularly, by name, desiring him and her and him to know of Jesus and to be brought under his wing, then you will speak *to* them. You will look them in their eyes. You will shape the story to include them, sometimes using their names. But you won't do these things because this is how stories are told, as if you were practicing a craft (and so paying more attention to a right method than unto the living kids before you). You will do these things spontaneously, *not* even thinking of them, because you have the hearts of these children upon your own pastoral heart.

Work with your strengths. Use music or drawings. But under-stand and honor the ancient oral tradition, since this has ever been the primary means by which one generation prepared the next to bear the mantle unto the third.

3. The Second Year: Know God
This was the year of hard work. But by this year we had estab-lished and nurtured a genuine partnership in the faith. So much of what it means to be human had already passed between us, so strong had our bonds become, and so common now was the base

upon which our hard work would stand, that we were ready for the hard work.

During this year I expected and received serious study: they memorized the biblical words which last year had been biblical stories for them; so they were not memorizing in the dark, as it were, isolated portions of Scripture. They were memorizing things already beloved and familiar.

I taught them according to Luther's Small Catechism—yes, just as I myself had been taught. But as we discussed a particular doctrine (say, the commandments) I would ask *them* to tell *me* the Bible story that supported our lesson (say, the story of the Golden Calf as example of idolatry). Their participation delighted the both of us, and I could praise them, and joy *did*, you see, prevail in these classes, even when learning was most difficult.

I went through the teaching material twice that year. First, for two-thirds of the year, teaching by means of homework, responsory activities, testing, methods common to any schoolroom.

Such labor required a truly communal support. Now, therefore, I called in the covenants of families and Baptismal sponsors, sending them a second set of the materials which the child was working on, asking them to set regular periods for working together at home.

The confirmation sponsors which each child chose I had installed in a public worship service in September. But to empower their support, I met with them as a whole group three times throughout each year, teaching them *how* to be sponsors; how, for example, to listen to memorization and comment on homework; how (especially!) to take their charges on private excursions during which the adult might share his or her own faith with the child, explaining by personal example *how* the faith is woven into the daily life of the adult.

After Easter of the second year (confirmation classes always continuing to Pentecost Sunday) the students planned, prepared, and served a fancy dinner in thanksgiving to their sponsors; for it was now, through the last third of the year, that we were reviewing the catechism material for the second time, studying furiously for the public examination.

4. Public Examination

Now, finally, came crunch time and the genuine rite of passage into spiritual adulthood: the moment of confirmation.

The nervous fear that preceded the public examination was good! It was necessary for the catechumen's sense of personal achievement. An initiation ritual is only as real as the task is real, as significant as the task is difficult. If it's free—or else made easy for the poor child—that child remains even in her own estimation a child still, and dependent. Moreover, expressions of faith that require no labor will carry no weight. To love and to honor the Lord will seem a light thing indeed—and shields so lightly constructed can protect against no weighty enemy after all, nor sin, nor death, nor the Devil.

So I gave them a genuine question-and-answer exam, seeking the doctrines now in their own words, from their own mouths.

But by now they did not see me as the cruel task's *master*. I was their helper! I, together with their sponsors, worked and worked the material into their hearts by saying: "We won't let you fail in front of so many people. We are on your side. You will strike them with astonishment by your great learning!" I became the managing coach. Their chosen sponsors worked individually with each. We made confirmation day into something like the final game of a long season.

At the same time we prepared the families likewise to take seriously the event to come. Plan parties, we begged. Invite relatives even from far away. This event must supercede birthday celebrations. It must be of greater moment than the prom (or what are we saying to our children about the things that truly deserve their hearts?).

In our church the public examination took place on the Saturday night before the Pentecost. All those supporting the confirmands attended. Family, sponsors, the officers of the congregation, all the teachers and every member who wished to come.

We chose an evening in order to have time for true questioning and careful answering. Everyone dressed up, for this was a formal affair, after all.

And when the confirmands had succeeded in their answers, when all teaching and all questioning were finally at an end, the adults who loved and honored the children now burst into a downright jamboree of laughter and applause. Always! Every year they whistled and stomped, though in each new year the applause was completely spontaneous and offered to that year's group alone.

Only once in all the rest of my tenure at Grace (from 1974 to the late 80's) did a student *not* pass.

On Pentecost Sunday itself, the final act of Baptism/Confirmation took place before the entire congregation.

"You are my child," the Lord had said, and made it true in the saying. Now that child, having come to understand the meaning of so celestial adoption, declared before the witness of the whole church, but unto none but Jesus himself, "And you are my Lord!"

No fears this Sunday morning. Only the joy of a sacred ascension, the self-confidence of personal accomplishment, the security of a new covenant uttered and established—and *well* established, given the difficulty of the task that brought the child to this first level of adulthood.

For salvation is free indeed. But discipleship has ever been a costly thing.

Pastors! Teachers, instructors in the Christian faith: soon the child before you will be my own, my grandchild, I mean, fresh and ready to be shaped by your training. I trust you with this bone of my own, that you shall not crush the joy in him, that you shall not merely entertain her. I expect the language of salvation to be as sober and as lively as is the business of salvation itself.

Please: do well by my children. Grant them adulthood in the Church that as adults they may be citizens of the Kingdom.

LITTLE LAMB,
WHO MADE THEE?

A Preface to "Little Lamb, Who Made Thee?"

I sat with the daughter and her father in the lounge of the youth and children psych ward in Wellborne Hospital. We occupied a corner, the father and I side-by-side on a short sofa, his daughter's chair at right-angles to ours.

The girl, however, could scarcely keep her seat, wriggling, wreathing her arms, tucking her legs up under her. She was a sophomore in high school, plain, roundish, with a Victorian abundance of brunette hair. I will call her Sharon here, though any other name but her own seems strange to me, and somewhat sad. It should not be that in public places I cannot call her by the name she knows for herself and herself inhabits.

Sharon dropped from her chair as if suddenly falling out of it. I made a spontaneous reach. Her father sat impassively. But Sharon had dropped to her knees, in fact, and was shuffling toward her father smiling brightly: all is well! All is well, and the daughter loves her daddy very much.

The man beside me did not move as she approached him. He wore a full beard. He sat like Lincoln, staring forward—staring still when Sharon lay her chin upon his knee and gazed up at him. In a moment she giggled and twisted around to sit on the floor with her back against his shins.

The lightness of her manner and the sweet persistence of her chatter—altogether as if they were cuddling of an evening in the living room—hardly fit the circumstances, unless of course she had recovered with wondrous speed and the cause of admission to the hospital were truly an aberration.

Sharon's father moved. He leaned slightly down to his daughter and reminded her that they were in a public place.

"Sit in your own seat," he said.

The man had eyes so intensely blue, they seemed to flame like gas jets.

Sharon jumped up, twirled on one toe and dropped hard into her seat.

These were almost the only words this father had for his daughter. He leaned back into his Lincoln stare, and I wondered whether he were profoundly disappointed in the child for her wretched carelessness. Sharon herself showed no disappointment whatever, neither in herself nor in her father's silence.

But she had only this morning, in the bathroom of Bosse High School, tried to kill herself.

The family had moved to Evansville only a few years earlier. Sharon's attempted suicide suggested to me that there may be certain interior stresses for which they may one day be willing to receive some help. So Thanne and I made a point to befriend them all, the parents and their two children.

But at that particular crisis, it was explained to me that Sharon was by nature high-strung and troubled. (Hence, I supposed, the serenity with which the father visited his daughter in the hospital.) She had, they said, been undone by the move from one state to another at about the worst time in her adolescence. She felt alien among the students at Bosse, bedeviled, belittled, terrifically unhappy.

Thanne's relationship with Sharon's mother took a true root; friendship bloomed between the two of them then.

My relationship with Sharon's father, although warm, remained rather formal. He was the pastor of a small congregation. It was perfectly natural for us to discuss professional issues; it gave me good cause to be near him, offering support without seeming to demean his own independence. The weight, the difficulties of his ministry presented themselves as complaints and criticism rather than as problems seeking thoughtful solutions or as weakness seeking companionship. Colleagues I think we were, or so I characterized the relationship. We never did, however, relax into the honesty of friendship. We never did become friends.

And then, when his daughter was a junior, the man announced to his wife and to his congregation that he was filing for divorce. Within a week he had moved out of the house into an apartment. I still met with him, but only in the pastoral office at his church. And Thanne, who in those days managed my writing and speaking affairs, offered his wife work in the office on the second floor of our home. It granted the woman a communal shelter and some money of her own.

And then, bare months after her father's departure, Sharon tried in bloody earnest to kill herself a second time.

Again the father and I met his child in the hospital. In no lounge, however. Beside her bed. And the girl bore bandages of comic thickness. But there was no coquetry in her face or in her manner. There was, rather, a pleading and a piteous sorrow.

And still the man was no more to her than a stone-white monument of the dead cerulean gaze. I bent to take the child's hand. I knelt to put my presence on a level with hers. And so it was that someone took her hand, but it was not the one she wanted, and it did not brighten her eye with life.

I left the hospital with a throat-full of suspicions.

That night I told Thanne what I was fearing.

And Thanne confirmed the worst.

Sharon's father had abused his daughter sexually. The move to Evansville had been the family's effort at a new beginning. The results of that effort were now sadly manifest. All these things Thanne had learned from Sharon's mother—because Thanne had recognized the symptoms long before I did, and had questioned kindly, softly.

How furious I felt that night! How dear to me was Sharon's broken self. With what tenderness I yearned to protect her deep, submerged and sacred beauty—to raise it up and praise it and persuade her of its truth.

All my life I've wished I were less passionate. Perhaps New York would not have dismissed me as a babbler then, or San Francisco as merely "emotional." Writers as uncontrolled as I lack the distancing irony that saves them from the world's contempt. Compulsively we do, and then we're forced to suffer what we did.

On the night of Sharon's second attempt, my passions governed me, and I wrote the letter printed below. I meant to give it to Sharon as soon as she was healthy enough to read it, and then I would offer myself as flesh and spirit to stand by the words, to stand by her.

Come the morning, however, and I repented of my plans. On the one hand, the letter seemed too brazen, too direct; on the other, it seemed too complex for a teenage mind. So I put it on Thanne's desk upstairs, hoping for her cooler opinion. If she feared its effect, I'd trash it.

Thanne did not read it. I mean, she was not the first to read it.

Having come in for work that afternoon, Sharon's mother found it. And though I had neither named her daughter nor specified the letter's intended recipient, as she read it the woman knew. She knew it belonged to Sharon. Without a word, then, and without my knowledge, she took the letter to her daughter.

Who read it herself.

And who, through her mother, sent serious thanks back to me. Sharon hadn't the words, yet. Abuse steals the most personal languages, and someone has to learn how to speak truth and truths and truly all over again. But Sharon had the experience, the effect, of an epistle that brings the better Shepherd to that one lost lamb; and of that experience she knew thanks, and these she sent to me.

In less than three months, while Sharon was still a teenager, but when she began to reveal signs of an uncommon maturity, she herself suggested that I publish the letter. Except for that it would have remained Sharon's own forever.

But I did. I published it in the regular column which I wrote in those days, for The Lutheran *magazine, which had a circulation then of some three quarters of a million readers.*

I published it thus:

Little Lamb, Who Made Thee?

Secretly beaten.

Sexually abused—

O child, it's not your fault. You do not have to earn the approval of your tormentor—no, nor his forgiveness either!

Is it strange that a victim thinks she caused the wrong and must right it again? Well, not so strange when we consider her helplessness. She's looking for leverage. She needs some principle by which to control her horror. And if *her* sin caused the punishment, then *she* might prevent it by a confession. See?

So the victim seeks her own iniquity—and the Christian faith is made grotesque thereby, allowing the guiltless to suffer guilt. And the abuser's become a Destroyer therefore, both of the body and the soul.

No, child—it was his act.

He was its cause. He was its doer. He took the wretched benefit. He must own it now, not you, not you.

He did it!

But because of your native innocence (which your tormentor encourages, since it shifts his guilt to you), and because you crave order in dangerous chaos (some ethical order anyway), you see a connection between one's behavior and one's fate. The good get goodness back again; and the bad get hurt—and look what a mess you're in; therefore you must be bad. Is that how you think? It saves the world from absurdity, doesn't it? It argues a certain rationality in human affairs. Good is rewarded, evil is punished, right? And your punishment proves evil in yourself, right? *WRONG!* Absolutely, unequivocally wrong.

If you've suffered abuse, the one who abused you sinned.

Sin is an uncaused evil. Responsibility sticks with the sinner. The sin came from him. He is the source. He bears the blame. His is the shame. Not you! Not yours! Do you hear me?

You, my child; you, dear lamb—you are beautiful and clean.

This sin occurred because a fool considered himself superior to you. He considered his whim superior to your health, his desire superior to your body, his mood superior to your peace. But you were made in the image of God, so his action condemns him: he demeans the creature whom God exalted; he attacks the child whom heaven loves. Listen: such spiritual blindness, such bestial selfishness, such a pitiful lack of self-control, declares this fool your inferior after all. You needn't seek kindness from him. No, no, and you need not forgive him either! For the Church that tells you you *must* forgive has burdened you with your sinner's sin, has laid a more terrible law on you, for you are not God, and you need not prove your Christianity now. You need prove nothing, not now when healing is the holy thing.

Let this fool seek forgiveness where it may be found; let him confess to the One against who he sinned most and most wickedly; let him confess unto Almighty God, for it is God who speaks for you now, child. And it is there that he can no longer excuse himself or compromise the force of his sin. It is there— and only there, finally—where he must strip his spirit bare and fall utterly on heaven's mercy and so be deeply and radically converted.

You need not, because you cannot, transfigure this fool.

God will, if the sinner wills. And the sinner must will! For *somewhere the sin must stop!*

The sinner tells me that it was his parents' fault in the first place. His father did him the same way. His mother was silent and critical. He didn't (he tells me) have a chance. He can't help his breeding and his personal shaping.

But if this is true, then we're all a cosmic landfill for every sin that ever occurred; they fall on us from the past generations, all the way back to Cain. Such a weight of sin (everyone else's fault except our own) must crush our innocent souls. Such an undeserved history must kill us.

But it hasn't killed us. In other words, there must be some break in this chain of responsibility, sinners causing sinner to sin—abusive parents turning their children into abusive parents.

And there is: it is the acceptance of responsibility *by the sinner,* by none other than the sinner himself, so that when divine forgiveness transfigures that one, the sin and the sinning are canceled together, and the chain breaks.

No, sir, it doesn't do to blame another, neither the parents before you nor the child behind you. You, sir, as perpetrator of a vile abuse, must with a contrite heart confess.

And you, the child whom he ravaged, must not call yourself ugly. You aren't. His action does not define you.

You, child: you are as soft as the blue sky. Touch your cheek. Do you feel the weft of life there? Yes: God wove you more lovely than wool of the clouds, smoother than petals of lily, sweeter than amber honey, brighter than morning, kinder than daylight, as gentle as the eve. Listen to me! You are beautiful. You are beautiful. If you think you're ugly, you've let a fool define you. Don't! Touch your throat. It is a column of wind and words. Stroke your forehead.

Thought moves through its caverns. Imagination lives in there. You are the handiwork of the Creator. You are his best art, his poem, his portrait, his image, his face—and his child.

And if the Lord God took thought to create you, why would you let a sinner define you?

God caused the stars to be, and then bent low to make you.

God wrapped himself in space as in an apron, then contemplated the intricacy of your hands; he troweled the curve of your brow; he fashioned the tug of your mouth and the turn of your tongue; he jeweled your eye; he carved your bones as surely as he did the mountains.

God conceived of time and in that instant considered the purposeful thump of your heart—and the blink of your eyelid.

God made galaxies and metagalaxies, the dusty infinitude of the universe—then filled your mind with dreams as with stars.

You are not an accident. You were planned. You are the cunning intention of almighty God. Well, then, shall you think ill of yourself? NO! You shall think as well of yourself as you do of any marvel of the Deity.

Please, my sister, do not allow a sinner to steal you from yourself. You are too rare. No matter what filth has befouled you, your soul is unique in the cosmos. There is none like you. Whatever thing you admire—a leaf, a little cup, a sunset—you are more beautiful.

Sleep peacefully, you. God loves you. And so do I. And so ought you in the morning light, when the dew is a haze of blue innocence. But sleep now, child, in perfect peace. You are God's, who spreads wide, holy wings above you now.

A Postscript to "Little Lamb, Who Made Thee?"

Within days of the publication of this letter, I began to receive mail from readers. I had never received so many responses to a single piece before. A rule of thumb is that one angry letter represents three angry readers; but one letter of agreement represents 10, nine of whom did not write.

Evening after evening, Thanne and I stood in our kitchen while I read the letters aloud. And we wept.

For there were more than a hundred letters in the space of three weeks.

And all but one were from women; and only one of those took issue with the column.

They told their stories, these women did in letters addressed to me. Handwritten, typed, printed from a computer. Countless stories of personal grief, the willful destruction of their persons and their personalities. They had BEEN the nameless. Yes, and it was their stories that made us cry.

But more than that, it was their courage.

For not one letter was sent nameless to me!

Woman after woman poured forth her terrible secret, then signed her name to it and did no longer hide. That gesture, so fearless, overwhelmed me with the sense of their resurrections.

No, I am not nor ever shall be ironic. Objective. A mind above the mass of human entoilment and experience.

Still, therefore, even now as I recount the deep entrenchment of this sin and its sorrow among us, I am borne down by the weight of it all.

And still I am dumbfounded by the valor of those who did not die.

My dear, dear friends: I take my own hope and courage from you.

From Sharon, too, who lives her life today in the company of her husband and their three children.

ALL THE ASSAULTED

i.

If you were not so frightened, child,
    As I am gentle, or . . .
If *I* were crouched, wide-eyed, defiled,
    And *you* the comforter,
    Then I would touch you.

But since it is that you've grown scared
    Of men, and since it is
That I have seven years, now, cared
    For you, I will not kiss
    You, child. Let that be true.

Let that be true along with this:
    That when you fall asleep
I wonder if an old man's kiss
    Would wake you. Oh, I'll keep
    That wish still unfulfilled—
But still will wonder, wonder still—
Oh, grandchild!—what a touch would do
If it were mine for touching you.

ii.

No. Sing another song.
Tell her a certain line
Between her brows ("a Rubicon
For deepness") is a sign.

Tell her you know how cruel
The grief within her is.
But you'll conclude it with a jewel:
And on that line, a kiss.

119

THE PARENT OF HIS CHILDREN

SNOWBOUND

IT WAS THE SNOWFALL of '76 (though I confess I'm fuzzy on dates and it might have been in '77).

January. The children were small, four of them, ages two to six. We lived in the country on two acres with chickens and fruit trees and large gardens. We were bordered by woods on the east and the south; to the west lay a farmed field; we shared the northern border with a neighbor who kept horses.

To this day the children remember a beautiful mare who slipped into a ditch and broke her leg. She had to be shot. They were the ones who discovered the accident. They stood at the edge of the ditch and watched the poor beast whinnying, lying like an eighteen-wheeler on her side, throwing her head up as if to snap her great body upright, rolling her eye so that the white showed terror.

This was new and horrible for my four young ones. Horses should not be helpless. Hugeness should not lie down and die. They came to the house with a look of awe in their faces. And then we heard the gunshot.

But that was a summer sometime after the winter of '76.

And that winter was kinder altogether, bequeathing unto us a snowfall of memorial proportions. It shut down the city for a week. Us it kept isolated for a full two weeks.

The storm began as a true blizzard, wind and a straking of snow straight out across the land. Our house leaked air, so it whistled and shuddered all night long. The boys, the older of the four, kept their eyes wide open. They had high, piping voices in those days. I heard them talking off and on about the relative strengths and weaknesses of the house.

"Joe? Joe? Is it goin' t'blow the baf-room away?"

"No, Matt, 'cause how would we pee then?"

"Oh."

By morning the wind had relented, but the snowfall itself continued down and down, and the world was utterly white. Cloaked, Siberian, forgiven. (*Though your sins be as scarlet, they shall be white as snow.*) All the ruddy, rotting colors of an exhausted autumn, all the blackened, unraked leaves, the shivering stalks in the beanfield, the corrupted melons in my garden—all was covered in a smooth white purity.

The children knelt at the window, transfixed.

God had called forth a new Eden.

"Can we," they whispered.

Their tiny voices were hushed by holy things. It sounded as if they were praying.

"Can we go. . .out?"

Going out, of course, was not without danger. Pigeon Creek snaked through the woods east and south on its way to the city. Hunters prowled the wooded banks, banging at living things. Not in January, though. Other months, other days. One once mistook my dog for something wild and free.

And once, after the creek had—in a quick succession—first flooded and then frozen, the boys snuck into the woods to explore the dazzling ice-world.

That afternoon their mother in her kitchen slowly became conscious of a distant sound, a faint cry, a sort of creaturely squeaking like fox kittens caught: "Mommy?" one voice mewed. "Mommy, mommy, mommy!"

The other voice barked, "Mop!"

Well, in those days Matthew was testing toughness. Tough kids don't say Mommy, and he never got the hang of Mom.

MOP!

Thanne ran down the hill and into the wood and found her sons stranded on a single circle of ice fixed like a tutu round the trunk of a large tree. The flood had begun to retreat. The rest of the ice, hollowed now, had broken under the boys' weight. "Mop?" They genuinely thought they would drown, tender adventurers paying for their boldness. Who knows how long they stood on the frost-island, crying?

But that was another year, another time.

Now they gazed upon a white paradise, soft, untroubled, a bosom mounded, maternal, abundant. Lo, as far as the eye could see through textured air the silent snow still coming down, the world was religious in serenity.

"Can we go. . .out?"

My chickens found the drifts impossible to negotiate, too deep for their legs, too high for flight. The effort defeated them. They were plumped here and there like marshmallows in milk, their wings having made angel-wings in the snow at their sides. If I had not myself gone forth, booted and gloved and blowing clouds, to bear them back to the coop, and if I had not then shut the door against their next escape (well, to them it was day, and day demanded foraging, and the instant they were returned to the dry coop they forgot the trouble with snows), they would have starved and frozen and died.

"Dad? Dad, can we?"

"What?"

"You know—go out?"

"Why?"

"To play."

In that same blizzard of '76 certain cattle were caught out in the fields, enduring alone the long night and the terrific blowing cold. They turned their backs to the wind; they packed themselves side-by-side together; they drooped their great heads. By morning the hoarfrost of their breathing had grown big and joined the earth, trapping their snouts in heavy columns of ice. Such silent, obedient monuments, bowed down, locked to the frozen ground, patiently dying.

But that was far west of us, out on the plains. Cattle in Southern Indiana are always closer to barns; and children are safe. The children are safe. Their parents protect them and keep them safe.

"Well, can we, Dad? Is it okay to go out and play?"

My oldest son ran away from home once. He slipped out the back door and headed west on a dusty road. He got as far as the bridge over the creek. A neighbor spotted him and drove him home again. He said afterward that he was looking for us because we had left and left him with an uncle who truly frightened him—so he lit out, though he was only four years old.

Even the little ones know of danger. And I think they suspect that something like death can descend on the living. They can be frightened. Their parents, of course, do more than suspect. Parents know in the cold part of their hearts that children can die.

"Yes," I said. "Yes, you can go out to play."

Grins bloomed in four faces, four little foxes whose expressions should never freeze in fierce grimaces—no, not these bounding and beautiful kittens.

"Wait!" I said. "Wait for me!"

Oh, my children, my children, so wonderfully young that winter! Oh, the radical magic of your innocence! In those days what you did *not* know transfigured the world I *did* know into something generous and kind and joyful and motherly and good after all.

This, then, is what I recall of the snows of '76: that we stomped a huge pie in a white field and chased each other down trails three feet deep and fell and laughed and blew clouds in frigid air and no one was hurt.

I remember snow forts in our snowbound days, each fort confronting the other, and snowballs stacked like cannonballs, and dusty throws of soft ammunition, and no one was hurt, and everyone felt the safety and the dearness of family.

I remember an ache in my wrist from the snow that crammed my mittens.

I remember an ache in my heart.

There was a snowman so huge that both my sons could stand on his hips to have their picture taken, their arms spread out like Hollywood stars, laughing, fearing nothing.

We ice-skated on Pigeon Creek.

For two full weeks we went out and played every day. And I loved my children until I wept. And not one of them was wounded. Not one.

But that was a very long time ago.

"MASTERPIECES!"

I WATCHED YOU SWIMMING, Mary. You were as unconscious of me as you were of yourself; but I was exquisitely aware of you—and then of myself as well.

Mary! You're not a woman yet, but womanhood is in you.

And suddenly, by slow degrees, the quality of my fatherhood is changing: new demands upon my soul, new dangers, revelations, new moments of the primeval quiet—and sometimes I'm a mumblin' fool with you, and sometimes I gaze in wonder like Balboa when he stood on an escarpment and contemplated the Pacific.

Mary, what are you doing to me?

What is happening to you?

The changes come slowly, to be sure; but we poor parents wake to them as though in surprise, and then we seek sympathy from companion parents, some consolation for the bewildering transformations of our children—while you children sometimes seem to take the whirling world so easily that we feel Paleolithic beside you. Sometimes, I say. For there are times when your limber spirit stiffens and brittles and breaks, and then you are like a figurine shattered, and no one can glue you, no, no one can put you together again.

Yesterday I watched you swimming in a blue Wisconsin lake—you, seabird, all alone. I sat some twenty feet above you on a bluff and so could see Olympian, as it were, could see through the lake to its bed below you, whose stones you never touched: you stroked too well and lightly through the element. Child, you were delightful, flicking the water like a trout with liquid, familiar assurance—

But I caught my breath and leaned forward, the better to see. Mary! Your legs are so long! And strong. And they churned the water with luxurious competence. And the crystal water gave them a pale, aquatic cast—dreamlike, it seemed to me, and absolutely beautiful. Mary! When did you come to be so beautiful? There are true hips at the ascendant curve of those legs, and a slender waist where once a child threw out her belly, and brown and lithesome arms, and bold shoulders. And when you toweled yourself, your wet lashes joined together like black starbursts, radiating glory round your eyes—blue eyes, shooting lashes, and a laughing child! Oh, Mary, when did you come to be so beautiful?

And when did you begin to stop to be a child?

When did that woman commence whom only now I notice?

All at once! By slow degrees.

There was a period, five or six years ago, when your older brothers received more letters than usual from aunts and uncles who addressed them in formal terms: "Master" Joseph and "Master" Matthew Wangerin. Talitha was perplexed by a title she had never heard before.

"If boys are masters," your younger sister asked, "then what are girls?"

You solved the puzzle straightaway, as easy as swimming.

"Masterpieces!" you declared.

And Mom laughed at the aptness, since you are a piece of work yourself; and I laughed for three or four seasons; and you—you laughed for the pure pink pleasure of it all, the center of attention, a round cheesecake of a child, dumpling cheeks, not a cloud in your blue sky.

Well, now in these latter weeks I realize, sweet Mary, variation in that laughter. The weather's less stable than it used to be, isn't it?—and could change upon the instant.

Or, the laughter's eager still; you grin so hard, and your eyes desire to swallow the one you're laughing with, and you clasp your hands at your breast (like any Victorian) never, never to let the sweet sensation go—

But suddenly, these days, a single word can change your aspect altogether. One frown from another can collapse the happiness and spill true tears down cheeks still formed for grinning. And the harder you laugh, the likelier are these tears to fall. High and low emotions are one with you, exultation and despair: you take offense as quickly as the snail's horns withdraw, and then my offended daughter, with her long strong woman's legs, storms up the stairs, wailing (a Victorian perfection of grammar), "You do not understand! No one understands me! I could just die—" And the bedroom door slams for punctuation, and you sail (in a graceful trajectory, surely) through the air and to your bed of bitterness, there to weep, "I could just die."

A woman nearly, nearly you are, a woman of complicated, intense, and profound emotions. No, you are not acting. This isn't pretence. Nor do you try on moods as people try on dresses to buy. The moods are painfully real in you, and life is less simple than it was. Relationships for you are in fact divine. Or else disastrous. And the divinity or the damage *does* last forever, until tomorrow. (I'm serious. I am not teasing you, my daughter. Today is forever in your baby woman's heart, and tomorrow is ever your wonder, unexpected when it doth come with healing in its wings.)

A woman you nearly, nearly are. But to me what are you truly, Mary?

My lover. (Oh, yes!) You comfort me in a manner most mature, having learned since childhood to read my moody meditations. Your eyes are perceptive. You see me truly, and quick to the heart; and your hand consoles me, even when lightly you pass me in the kitchen and pause in the passing; and you are beautiful in compassion. A woman. Such a woman.

But what are you to me?

A thunderstorm! A headache. (Oh, yes! So changeth the weather.) Suddenly things are not hard for you, nor merely difficult: they are *"impossible,* Father!" Anything I ask you to do, when you're convinced that you cannot or should not do it, causes you trauma—and formalizes me in the process, refusing me my more intimate names and freezing me with "Father." Then how do I reason with one who declares with creedal conviction that I "hate" her? One tormented by loneliness, lovelessness, as forlorn as the poet at the fading of his nightingale? One who sees me as the Ogre, the Ancient, both stony and hateful, the Judge, the Warden, and the Executioner?

I don't. I'm smarter than that. I do not try to reason with such a one. Simply, I wait for tomorrow, which, though you dispute the turning of the times, shall most surely come. I wait for tomorrow, when I shall be your intimate again, and your tender friend.

Ah, Mary, when did you begin to stop to be a child? It's a difficult business, isn't it, this adulthood. You yearn it and you curse it, woman.

When did you begin to cover yourself and lock the bathroom door against us? When did you begin to take yourself and all the world (and right and wrong, and justice and international oppressions) so seriously? And when did you become so beautiful?

All at once! By creeping, slow degrees.

God gave us a sky of infinite and wild variety, storms and the imperial blue, scudding clouds and the symphonic sunset and lightning too. But the sky never touched me lightly to say, "I love you." Nor could that sky receive my little love in return.

So God gave us daughters—

—more wonderful than the sky, lights for telling the seasons by.

Ah, Mary.

Masterpiece!

NO FIELDS OF YELLOW FLOWERS ANYMORE

i.

When our neighbor informed us that our small son could no longer play with her daughter, I was sorry, but I didn't argue. Rather, I took the opportunity to school him in self-restraint.

Even from infancy Matthew had been an exuberant child. Life and every desire were matters of gladness for him. He was up with the morning sun, loud and laughing and out the door, racing the fields like a sheepdog, loving the grass and the speed and the freedom. Oh, Matthew! He was three and free—never, never the slave of anyone or of anything.

We lived in the country in those days. I raised all sorts of fruits and vegetables. Matthew tended to the sweeter crop always—and when strawberries fattened in the green patch, he did not, as he said, "Think two times." He flew on wings of an aching hunger faster than anyone else, landing on hands and knees, ramming his face among the leaves.

I yearned to delight in life as he did.

At the same time I wished that he would learn self-discipline because he could hurt himself. He could hurt others, too—and he did, and he always felt remorse thereafter, and that was perhaps the worst way of hurting himself, but he did it again. He always did it again.

Ah, the wild child! There was such a splendid joy in his satisfactions. Unrestrained in action, he was also unrestrained in gladness—and then again as unrestrained in sadness when his natural self would wound another. It all went together, you see? Desire and delight and a native skill gave Matthew the edge: so he got there first; he ate it first; he ate it *all*, thinking of nothing but the fat red strawberry bursting its sugarjoy against his palate—until there was none left for others. Nothing for his family. Nothing for his three-year-old friend, who may have felt frightened by such energies both going and coming.

So, then, I didn't argue when her mother announced the new rule: "Your son is out of control," she said, and she ended the friendship. The children were forbidden to visit. No more playing. No talking, no whispering secrets. Nothing.

Matthew was suddenly very sad when I told him this law. He really liked the girl, this tiny porcelain person so different from himself, small-boned, wispy-haired, blue veins in a milk-white skin. His eyes grew large and silent in sadness, and I took the opportunity to teach:

"You've got to think of other people first, Matthew," I said, "or look what happens. People go away." We stood in our backyard, he gazing across the new, invisible wall, I gazing down at him. "Matthew, give before you take. Walk before you run. Listen before you talk, and whisper before you shout."

But he kept gazing next door.

He murmured, "Now but she don't have a friend too, either."

"I guess not," I said.

"My fault," he whispered.

I held my peace.

He looked up at me. "Daddy, can I take her a bowl of strawberries?" *Daddy, can I fix the friendship?*

"Not now," I said. "We don't have any ripe strawberries left, remember?"

He kept looking at me. "Well, maybe later," I said, thinking that Matthew's lesson might honestly change him, and the change in him might change our neighbor's mind. Maybe she'd relax her law in the future.

I was wrong on every count. Worse: I was deceived, and when the truth appeared I saw in it the dangerous intransigence of the imagination of the human heart.

Within the month my wife telephoned me at the office. "Come home," she said. She was crying. Thanne seldom cried. "Please come home right now," she said. "I found out why Mrs. Duvall cut Matthew off from her daughter—"

"Because he's hyperactive," I said.

"Please," Thanne sobbed, "just come home."

I did. I drove home. I listened for ten minutes to Thanne's explanation, hearing how wrong I could be. My blood rose up in fury. I went straightway to the house of our neighbor and, with restraint, confronted her. She answered in civil voice. In fact, she spoke in a smiling conspiratorial tone, as if two intelligent adults such as ourselves would agree on a matter like this. She felt no need to explain nor to apologize—no, not even to feel guilty. But Thanne's information had been absolutely accurate. And the way this woman accepted so serenely my burning accusation, the complete ignorance of any wickedness in all of this, astonished and aggrieved me—which dead-sorrow of soul I have not forgotten even to this day.

I came home and looked for my son. I found him downhill behind the house in a field full of yellow flowers, his arms flung out to some interior melody, turning circles. Actually, the flowers were a kind of weed in poor soil, profuse that summer; but to me they seemed most terribly beautiful for that my son was in their midst, and my heart was smitten thereby. The yellow field seemed a sort of grounded sunlight, a glory around his dark complexion.

Oh, Matthew!

I descended to him, then knelt in the field, and gathered the boy in a hug so tight he grunted.

"Daddy? Daddy, what's the matter?"

"Well, let's keep our strawberries here. We'll eat them together. But I don't think we should take them next door. Not now. Not ever."

Matthew had huge brown eyes. "Why?" he said. "Don't they like strawberries?"

He didn't understand. Nor, at that age, could he. In time he would, of course; but then he would be more than sad. The boy would be confused and wounded personally; and by then he'd know that he was suffering the assaults of a most iniquitous world.

ii.

Parents, we teach our children fairness; and we do well.

The selfish child is a danger. The self-centered child grows into a marauding adult whose sins are justified by that same grim idol, *Self.*

We wish our children to be good, and so we teach them to be just; to be selfless themselves; to do to others as they would have others do unto them. We teach them to be fair.

We do well.

And we do it (don't we?) out of deep parental fears and affections. We train them in fairness for their own protection, because we do not want them to suffer blame or slaps hereafter, do we? In a world both bigger and badder than they are, selfish children are dangerous mostly to themselves.

So we take every opportunity to say: "Don't be selfish. Share with your friends, and they will stay friends with you." Cause and effect, right? While buttoning their coats for school, we say, "Play by the rules, kid, and others will learn to trust you. They will *like* the one who knows right from wrong and acts upon it." Connections, right? Good people do good; good invites good friends; goodness gets goodness in return. We drive our youth to college, repeating the fine and fundamental ethic: "Be fair, son, even when I'm not near to watch you. O my dear daughter, out of your own soul, be fair. This is moral independence. This is maturity. When you practice fairness, you are on your own finally and surely. Be fair."

In this way we imply that they have a personal control over their destinies: certain behaviors will have certain consequences. Choose the right behavior for a righteous future. All we teach them is based upon the presumption that there is a reasonable law at work in the world—reasonable and feasible and universal and impartial: *The Law of Fairness.*

Its positive expression is this: Good behavior earns a good reward. Good gets goodness in return. This is a most consoling logic, both for the parent and the child.

Its neutral expression is: If you do not misbehave, you will be left in peace.

And its negative: But if you break the law, the world will punish you according to your deserving. Ill deeds bring an ill response. This may be a cold logic, but it is orderly withal and necessary.

The Law of Fairness does not pretend to love people; rather, it loves stability in the community, and everyone benefits. It maintains a structure that all can understand, within which every individual can choose good or evil for himself. Its very rigidity, therefore, permits a moral liberty person by person, gives ethical independence to child and child, no child excepted.

See? In any game—in this game particularly—it's good that there are rules, and good to know the rules, and good that the referees are watching the rules. Each individual may now play heartily, and the winner *is* a winner after all.

So we teach our children *The Law of Fairness* as carefully as we can, both to know it and to obey it. And we do well thereby; and all should *be* well therefore.

And all *would* be well—if the world itself obeyed that law.

But what if the world the children encounter tears fairness to shreds? What then?

iii.

At ten-thirty on a Saturday night Matthew was just coming out of a gas station door, his head down, counting change, when he heard shouts by his car.

He looked up. Two police officers were pointing stern fingers in the faces of his friends. His friends were backpedaling, helpless.

One of the officers shouted: "Get in the car! Get in the car right now!"

This, Matthew knew, was not possible. By habit he'd hit the button that locked the doors. Even as he broke into a trot toward the gas pumps, he heard the cop continue: "Get in, boy, or you're going to jail!"

Exact quotes (though not unlike other quotes he has heard often and often). Matthew doesn't forget what he meets with emotion. His mind and his heart are strong.

He pulled the car keys from his pocket as he approached the scene. The officer saw him and redirected the order. To Matthew, now, he yelled, "Open this car. Get in and get out of here, now, *now!*—or you're the one going to jail!" Matt's the one. My son is the one.

He was seventeen years old. (But it happened when he was sixteen. It has happened every year of his driving life.) He had by then developed a flat manner for precisely this sort of situation. That is, he blanked his eyes and slacked his face and slowed all motion until nothing in him suggested threat, aggression, or flight. He stared into the air. He neither grimaced nor smiled nor said, "Sir." Any such gesture is dangerous.

Deliberately Matthew began to unlock the four doors of the car—

And the uniforms exploded: "Not fast enough. I don't like your attitude, boy! In fact, show me ID. Now, now, NOW!"

Just then a friend whom the police hadn't seen stepped round the car, surprising them. "Yow!" They both leaped backward snatching their sidearms. Embarrassed, they yelled, "Oh, yeah! Oh, yeah, you are going to jail!"

Matthew stood absolutely still, now *not* giving back what he was getting nor getting what he had ever given; now *not* invoking fairness nor anticipating it nor even believing in it—for he had learned, Lord; he had learned beyond my teaching him; he had learned that the best posture in a crisis like this is not to be. Vanish.

Matthew had learned by cruel and redundant experience.

I do not lie. I declare it as an objective fact that my son has regularly been harassed by officers of the law for no ill that he has done and in spite of the good that he has sincerely chosen.

My son is adopted.

He is black.

His color alone is, in this world, the cause of his harassment.

iv.

We live now in a black neighborhood, in the center of our city, where there is the congeniality of community for our children.

The police here are mostly white.

But we were not wrong to move here. Here most of the people suffer the same derisions of *The Law of Fairness,* and here we can talk of the trouble to folks who understand it in their bodies as well as in their minds.

While we still lived out in the country, we experienced the cold, white eye alone; and we, at first, were inclined to accept guilt. Well, we hadn't yet learned. We didn't recognize the depth of human prejudice nor the bland face it wore. We thought it was we and our children who were somehow at fault. We (Thanne and I in our own belated ignorance) were still assuming fairness to be an active principle of human relationship—

—until our neighbor spoke the truer motive of her mind.

That's why I hugged my son so hard and why he looked so terribly beautiful and tragic in the field of yellow flowers. The mother of his young friend had just said to me, without anger but with a complete and creedal conviction: "They won't never talk again 'cause black and white don't marry."

That was the reason for the separation.

She said, "I don't want them touching or holding hands or whispering secrets. It's unnatural. You go on and keep him hobbled and at home, away from my girl, 'cause black and white don't—"

don't marry, she said, when these two children were no more than three years old. And she smiled as if I would surely understand the long weight and history of her truth.

But this was truth: that *The Law of Fairness* crumbled in the face of such mindless, murderous racism.

The Law of Fairness was a far less effective ward in the wicked world than the "trick" that Matthew had learned thereafter, which is not to trust anyone, which is the blank expression, the slack face, and vanishing. Do nothing. Say nothing. Be nothing.

That night, when he was still seventeen, it worked. He seemed to the officers sufficiently subservient. He did not go to jail. He came home. He shrugged and told me the story, by then a very old story. No big deal. This is the way things are. Cops harass young black males.

But I wish he were three again, dark and lovely in a field of yellow flowers, laughing as once he laughed when he was innocent, when desire and delight and satisfaction and life were all one with him. Fairness was a good law then. And my son could hope and be happy then—

v.

All of our children must suffer the loss of that good law. Do you understand? The world is not, after all, fair.

So what do we do when it is the world and not our children which proves selfish in the real encounter?—selfish and unrepentant and unpunished after all?

Teachers will deal unfairly with our daughters; coaches will scream at our sons, pink and popeyed; friends will trash our children at the pleasure of other friends; bosses will play favorites; the marketplace will not love our children as we do, but will rather love itself at their expense; countless promises will be made and, though the children count on them, will then be broken. Politicians will lie. Police will obey the imagination of their hearts more than the cool and equable law. So what do we do when bad people possess power while good and goodness are crushed as wimp and weakness?

Injustice, in this fallen world, will certainly strike the child both bluntly and personally.

Listen, parents:

If we do nothing, if we do no more than communicate *The Law of Fairness* strictly and only, then our children will change to protect themselves, but the change will break our hearts.

One young man may react with an anger so radical that all our teaching—all of it!—shall be compromised and lost on him. He may then mimic the world, exchanging laws of fairness for laws of brutality: might makes right. The strong survive. Look out for number one, since you have no better friend than yourself.

Or one young woman, having been deceived, may never trust another person again. To the degree that she was burned for her faith in fairness, to that same degree she shall now doubt promises altogether and dread the motives of other people. Scared child! If hurt came from the place she had considered safe, then hurt can come from anywhere. And love itself becomes the ultimate personal risk—too dangerous ever to take. Lonely child, unfulfilled and frightened.

Or the saddest change within our children is this, that they never let go of *The Law of Fairness,* that they accept therefore the guilt and consider themselves deserving of all the hurt the world gives unto them. A harsh twist: they believe themselves evil precisely because they have had to suffer evil. And if they cannot perceive what wrong they did to cause it, soon they conclude that it is the wrong they *are.*

If, when this good law breaks in a broken world, we do nothing new for our children, they shall begin to die various early deaths.

vi.

At Bosse High School Matthew played the point position for his basketball team. He had the spirit of a leader. Even off the court he wove his players together by driving them hither and yon in his car, by giving them haircuts in our basement, by gathering the team together at our house before a game. I remember with pleasure the laughter bubbling from the basement, and I cooked suppers for them, and I felt a parent indeed.

All but two of the Bosse players were black.

I remember, too, how nervous the team would become on the days they had to be bused from the city into the counties of southern Indiana to play small-town high schools in all-white communities.

These plain folk in their own gymnasiums enjoyed a joke or two. When they met a team as black as Bosse's, their fans would enter the stands carrying hubcaps. Humor. Matthew and his teammates simply expected it. Students wore watermelon patches, red, green, and seeded. "Fun! It's all in good fun!" Yet, though he expected it, Matthew genuinely did not understand why this was considered funny, why folks laughed, why parents rocked backward on their seats amused. Oh, he knew that whites think that blacks like watermelon. But why such an unsubstantiated notion of one people regarding another should make the first people laugh, he had not a clue. But he tolerated these milder forms of foolishness. All the Bosse players did. Part of basketball. Hoosier hysteria. We live in Evansville on the Ohio River.

But then in the dark midwinter of 1988—just as the bus and its basketball team were slowing down to turn off Highway 231 into the parking lot of a rural high school—there flared beside the windows a sudden fire, a bright ascending yellow flame. Suddenly, boys could see boys' faces in the firelight, and the bus driver gunned his engine. Matthew's eyes went as wide as when he was young. The entire team fell silent, watching.

This was the first time any of them had seen a cross afire.

Matthew (he later told me) had such tightness in his chest he couldn't breathe. It occurred to him that a fire near a high school was unsafe. Even the building might burn.

So, then, how do you exit a bus in front of strangers? How do you strip and change clothes in foreign walls? How do you enter the glaring light and loud sound of a basketball court when your own mood is so filled with confusion? Well, the act had seemed so obscene to Matthew—that someone should burn the cross of Jesus. What had Jesus done? He couldn't make sense of it. His stomach was knotted. His face felt hot. Something was dreadfully wrong. But how do you walk on court when everyone else is happy, laughing, and ordinary?—though somebody in this place just torched the wood of the Christian cross.

Well, you enter stiff. Wooden-legged. You put on the blank-eyed mask of not-caring, the impenetrable wall and the slack-faced declaration that nothing matters. You pretend indifference even while your heart ticks so quickly you feel the pulse in your throat, and your ears are so acute that they hear the whispers, *Nigger, nigger.* But the word registers nowhere in your expression. You take the ball. You shoot. You warm up. Stretch. Avoid looking at the stands. Shoot. Shoot. Shoot.

vii.

There is another law. The laws of fairness and brutality are not the only ones a child might learn. Against these two—or against lawlessness altogether—the third is absolutely essential.

This is what we do when the children suffer the failure of fairness in the world: with all our hearts, for the health and the blessing of the children forever, we model before them and for them enact *The Law of Forgiveness.*

Parents, if we love them this is not a matter of choice. It is necessary for the life of the children. Without it, they shall be caught in a killing society, dying. Moreover, it is at the core of our Christian faith: a loving God knew the need long before we did. . . .

We who have been appointed parents by the most Holy Parent must in all our action image the forgiveness of Christ himself—and must name Christ Jesus both as the Lord and as the source of what we are doing. No secrets here. His forgiveness must pattern the children's. His forgiveness must empower theirs. And as their spirits more and more reflect the Spirit of God, they shall more and more be *free of the world*— neither to be ruled nor to be crushed by it.

This is not merely an abstract doctrine to be conned.

This is wholly pragmatic.

This is a daily shield, the children's best protection after all.

Even as we train them to eat and to dress and to perform some sustaining skill, so we must train them to sever themselves from the hurt and the powers of the world (though not from the world itself) by a true and holy pardoning.

Sinner, I do not hold this thing against you.

No, the children do not say such a thing simply on their own. They must know (by your guidance) that Jesus said it first to them from the cross, and that Jesus says it thereafter *through* them to the world before them.

Whisper their sins to their souls until they ache in sore repentance; but then quickly sing to them the measure of the mercy they have received the dear Lord. Their sins are gone. In place of sin is righteousness and the love of God. The Spirit of love then lives within them. God is there, and from the God in them truly, truly comes this miraculous power to forgive the people who do not in fact deserve forgiveness.

But forgiving inverts the powers. Evil cannot control those who do not fear evil; and those who forgive it do not fear it; they are above it, gazing *down* upon it in pity. Nor can evil rule those who are themselves not evil. Those filled with grace are filled with God.

Children of forgiveness are liberated, therefore, from this world, utterly free, making choices altogether on their own, unpressured, unthreatened, unambitious, unpersuadable. Such children enjoy partnership with the almighty God. The world can indeed destroy *The Law of Fairness,* but it cannot destroy that which dodges its tooth, *The Law of Forgiveness.* Why, it cannot comprehend the premise at all. Forgiveness is a puzzle before it.

Again, the world can destroy any child committed to *The Law of Brutality*, since the greater power may always kill the lesser. But it cannot destroy the Holy Companion of the child of forgiveness, nor else the child that this dear Companion keeps.

And look at the marvelous accomplishments of such children of the Spirit: they become the means by which God enters the world; for their forgiveness is the coming of Jesus again and again.

Is there a higher calling than to be the bearer of the Lord?

viii.

They won. Matthew's team won.

No razzle-dazzle, no slam dunks, no show—just a steady game, a solid and solemn, respectable win. The fans in the stands were not happy.

Neither was Matthew's coach, despite the triumph. He was nervous, tense—and finally furious.

As both teams were leaving the court, a heavy-set man sitting half-way up to the ceiling bellowed something about a "nigger win," and the coach of Bosse's team blew up. With a strangled shout he began to mount risers, clearing a path by short chops of his arms, preparing to crack the skull of a fat fan who was suddenly very frightened. Friends of that fan started to converge around him, balling their fists.

But immediately both basketball teams swept up the stand together, like sea waves.

And amazingly, Matthew was not afraid. He was the first to reach his coach. He tried to pull the short man backward and got tossed aside for his effort. But he wasn't scared, and he truly did not expect a fight—because of what had happened during the game.

The first half ended in a grim stand-off, a balanced score and an equal suspicion on both sides.

But near the beginning of the second half, Matthew (by habit, I think, a spontaneous act) complimented his opposite for a good shot. Just a nod, an acknowledgement between equals: "Hey, man."

And "Hey," said his opponent.

And suddenly Matthew realized the potential of the gesture. Several times by glances and touches he praised the white point guard. Since he himself was known as a good player, the compliment carried weight. And the opponent, not bad himself, smiled back, grinned back, praised Matthew in return.

So, then, there was a mutual relationship here, independent of the noises in the gym, shaped at first by a common commitment to the same game. So, then, Matthew's mask cracked and his hot face cooled. So, finally it became a conscious gesture on his part to forgive: to honor the humanity of the other, permitting the other as fully human also to return relationship.

The rest of the team observed in two point guards the lack of fear and vengefulness. They saw in Matthew a weird, uncaused behavior (except as God causes things that otherwise would never have happened, as God makes miracles through his children), and so they hunkered down and played basketball. Both teams shut out the idiocy of sinful fans and apoplectic coaches. They played the game they liked; and within this pale of forgiveness they liked the players they faced.

It was a good, close game.

That's why Matthew wasn't afraid when his coach arose in a rage and he himself went after him. It was a single team that swept up the stands and interposed itself between the Bosse coach and the friends of a fat fan—a single team composed in equal measure of white and black players, rural and city, Bosse and Bosse's opponents.

You see? *All* the players were, by the benefaction of the forgiveness of one, perfectly free.

ix.

Yesterday I said good-bye to my son all over again. He was on his way back to college. He is twenty. I feel a heartbreak homesickness for him.

He has, of course, changed. Innocence is gone. Likewise, his exuberance is much tempered—or else he'd get into trouble much more than he does. He is cautious now. And I am altogether helpless to protect him. No more. I cannot attack the attackers any more.

The sense of general fairness and universal beauty in this world has been compromised for both of us. Various sorts of worldly authorities accomplished that destruction.

Matthew departs this home of his parents for a difficult life, my dear one does. I hugged him. I hugged him very hard, but I could not hug him long, as once among the flowers. There are no fields of yellow flowers anymore.

I hugged him and let him go, and he is gone.

And now I console my loneliness in prayer:

O Holy Father of my son, he bears in your forgiveness his veriest strength. Forgiven, he can forgive—and forgiving, he shall survive this world unto eternity. Never let my boy forget this best of lessons. Never.

Amen.

DAUGHTERTALK

I WISH THE FISH took my bait as quickly as my daughter takes the ring of the telephone.

One ring and that child has burst from the bathroom, scorched through the kitchen, and snatched the receiver: "Hello, this's Mary."

One ring! Evidently there are no joys Mary will not forego for the phone. Certainly a long, contemplative, comfortable crouch in a little room is no match for a chat.

Mary doesn't like to be alone. My daughter's gregarious by nature and gladdest when gossiping.

Listen: the other night while she was sleeping—in her bedroom, an hour into her slumber, the door being closed where she lay— the telephone rang. Even before that first ring finished, Mary— sleeping still, her pupils as tiny as pinpricks, smiling in dreamy expectation—Mary went floating down the hallway: "I'll get it," she murmured.

I do not lie. I woke her before she embarrassed herself by sleep-talking.

Ah, but over the telephone that girl *never* embarrasses herself. She's a TJ for skill and aplomb, *Telephone Jockey,* liquid language, opinions on any matter, grace under pressure.

When Mary receives the heavy-breathers' call (as she has), she holds her own cheery conversation until *he* hangs up. "Hello? Hello? Hello?" she chirps. "Oh, poor pitiful-little-mute-man, what's the matter? Asthma? Can't you talk? You think maybe I'm nine-one-one?"—and so forth.

She is undisturbed even by the mentally disturbed, as long as her weapon is the telephone. Mary's an expert.

She's tireless, too.

Howcanateenagertalkforhoursandneverrunoutof*words*? Or out of breath either?

And are both of them talking at once? I mean, is the father of the daughter at the other end *also* hearing endless, breathless, uninterrupted news reports about nearly nothing at all? Or when does Mary's interlocutor get to speak?

Well, I believe these children have perfected a method of talk/listening whereby they do both at once with equal energy. I think there's a detachment within the head of the mouth from the ear. Just as, when teens do homework while watching TV, there's an obvious detachment between brain and face. It's an evolutionary phenomenon.

Progress.

Moreover, with the talk/listening method it is possible to attend to five, ten, twenty topics all at the same time. This is why teenagers can discuss seventeen significant issues while flying through the kitchen and out the back door: unkind teachers, no homework again, friends in life-and-death situations requiring immediate visits, don't wait up, and good-bye. While the poor parent, pop-eyed, is still emerging from the consolations of the bathroom and wondering if he heard the telephone ring.

Now, then, the posture for telephone calls will vary according to the caller and the urgency of the call.

They are as follows, depending on who's at the other end:

Girlfriends: Lie on the floor, feet propped on the walls, hair in disarray. Gesture with the free arm. No matter the clothing, no matter the lighting. This is the posture for gossip.

Girlfriends, pastime: Watch TV with the girlfriend on the line—two phones, two TV sets, two running sets of opinions, two bloody shrieks for brothers who, mistaking a phone call for a phone call, switch channels. Also, while watching TV and talk/listening, do one's nails—and blow on them too.

Girlfriends, serious: Sit up, hunch over, hang the hair around one's head as if in private, but speak dramatically, even explosively—especially if discussing some personal insult.

Boyfriends: Laugh a lot. Stand up. Prance, swinging the free arm wildly. Good lighting for glancing in mirrors.

Boyfriends, serious: Sit in a chair. Doodle with pencil or the forefinger. Button all buttons as if dressing well. Low light is preferable. Music too—but not MTV.

Boyfriends, very serious: Absolutely no one else in the room. If a parent should skirt too close to this lair, a hissing will indicate his danger.

Boyfriends, very, very serious: Perfect silence. Weeping.

This last posture the father will notice. He will wait until the call is concluded, and then he will offer his daughter a hug. She has run out of words. No TJ now, no longer tireless, no expert at anything—she is desolated. Her father holds her very tight and hates the phone right now. He hates anyone and any thing that hurts his daughter.

On the other hand, there is no punishment worse than being grounded with telephone silence.

Ask Mary.

For it is on the phone that she renews her spirit again, laughing. Oh, this child laughs at the fleetingest joke and, having started, cannot stop. Tinkling laughter runs into boisterous laughter swells into mighty Mississippis of laughter, till my Mary is left gasping and streaming tears over some fool thing one of them said, which is, of course, not funny in the retelling but which, in fact, is friendship anyway. Plain friendship. Whole and healthy, holy friendship.

And in such moments I love the telephone very much. I appreciate anything that makes my baby lovely again.

But I wonder, as I pass the poor kid squealing on the floor: are these two friends just moaning in one another's ear, saying nothing, yowling like animals? No words? No worthy communication on this expensive and advanced device, but inarticulate giggles and woofings as if they never learned language at all?

Is this what the phone has returned us to, the primitive grunt and the Mary-onic burble?

Actually, no: it's not the invention, it's the daughter. She'll do it off satellites and halfway round the globe; or else by wire; or face-to-face, if she has to. She'll do it cheap or dear—all's one with her.

She *must talk,* whether in words her parents recognize or in noises more expressive of the subtler teenage spirit, burps and barks and purrings.

However complex, however progressive technology may get, it is the daughter that does not change. For which pertinacity, saith this father (from within a small, locked, porcelain room, his only throne in a house inhabited by a Princess): *Praise the Lord after all.*

THE ALTAR OF
MOTHERHOOD

Deliberate, devout, and beautiful, the woman walks to the altar and places there her precious gift and watches while it is consumed—

How long has this been going on? For eons.

How many people have done it? Myriads. But mostly women.

Then why haven't we been astounded by such holiness? Well, I think we are by nature blind to sacrifice. Even the receivers of this outrageous love don't truly know its depth if they have never felt the wound of it, have felt the sweet blessing only. Perhaps we have to suffer sacrifice in order to understand it.

Perhaps that's why I didn't know my mother well. I mean: I didn't know the quality of her love until I myself experienced her circumstance and did myself make a mother's choices—

Children, honor that woman who for your sake placed on the altar of motherhood some core part of her precious self. Honor and do not neglect her!

In 1985 Thanne and I switched household duties. She went to work full-time, and because mine was the more mobile work, I brought it home. Writing had become my primary profession. Now housekeeping became my primary obsession. From that year forth I took over the cooking, the shopping, the kitchen, the bed, and the bedroom—yea, and the children.

Through the winter and spring of 1985 things went swimmingly. By eight in the morning I was alone in the house, busy in the kitchen, to be sure, but at the same time thinking through the day's writing ahead of me. By nine, dinner was in a crock and I was at the typewriter. For six solid hours thereafter, the writer wrote.

At three in the afternoon the children came home. So writing was done. The writer turned into a father, and the father emerged from his study ready to usher his children everywhere. I cheered their games, I refereed their arguments, I disciplined and pitied and talked and cooked and set the table and timed our dinner to begin at six, when Thanne got home.

Thus the noonday writer and the afternoon father thrived, both of them—so long as they stayed separate.

But then came June. And my dear children came home to stay.

Now, I had committed myself to completing a book-length manuscript that summer, but I trusted my ability to organize and I intended to accomplish the same amount of work now as I had when school was in session. I established a schedule to occupy the kids (with an equal mix of chores and recreation) while I wrote. Of course I would write. There never was a question about such a thing. I was a writer. That was my core *self,* my purpose for being.

But the telephone was suddenly seized with a thousand fits of ringing a day. And the children ate meals whenever the mood took them. And friends came over, shouting, fighting, laughing, interrupting the sweet symmetry of my schedule (chores and recreation). Okay, so I had to stop writing, come out of my study, put limits on the use of the phone, dismiss kids who were not my own, remind my own (over and over) to clean the kitchen after their meals, and stab my finger for emphasis at the schedule on the refrigerator: "Do, do, *do,* you fools!"

Back to writing again. Whew.

Ah, but even when I didn't rush out of the study, every time a kid raised his voice I had to stop. To listen. To figure out what was going on. Or any time the kids lowered their voices, I had to stop. To listen even harder. Silence is dangerous. And if you can't hear it, you have to go *see* it. So up and out I went after all.

And you cannot schedule arguments. And you can't plan tragedies. So? So I stopped writing. I burst out of my room. I yelled. I arbitrated. I held my poor daughter till she stopped crying. Ach, I stopped, and I stopped! I brought kids here, I drove them there, I answered their questions, I filled out their forms, I took them swimming, and I blew up:

"LEMME ALONE! JUST LET ME ALONE! I'VE GOT TO WRITE!"

("Shhh, Daddy's going crazy.")

Okay, so I stopped writing altogether. That is, I decided it was time for a whole new start, for all of us. I took a week's break from writing, calmed my spirit, jettisoned all that I had (so miserably) written during the first days of summer, quietly instructed the children in the necessities of my job ("It feeds you, sucker!"), and sat down to start all over again, refreshed—because, of course, I *would* start over again. I would surely write. It's who I am, you see—

Can anyone explain to me? Why, if you have told your children never to interrupt you, do they interrupt you with little whispers as if whispering were better? As if whispering proves them obedient after all? I HATE WHISPERING! IT DRIVES WRITER-DADDIES MAD!

Okay, so then why *don't* children interrupt you when they're about to take off for parts of the city you've never yourself had the temerity or the stupidity to enter? And why must the writer-daddy come out of his study to find the house as dead as marble? Wondering where his children have gone? And whether his previous rage is the cause of their present danger? Dumb, dumb, dumb, Daddy!

Three times that summer I stopped, cooled, smiled, gathered my forces, and started all over again. Three times my children slew the book in me. Three times!

But these kids were not bad kids. No, they were just plain kids who needed a parent. It's the order of things. They needed a presence. A mother. But I am so slow to learn. And finally, only experience itself teaches me. By bending me to the right will, the holy way.

Finally, I bowed my head before my children's natural need. Finally, I confessed in my soul, *This is right. These children of mine must take precedence—because they are children and they are mine and they come first—yea, though it consume me—*

Then, then I discovered my mother's mothering and the astonishing quality of her love. Then: when I chose. When I sacrificed the writer-self and consciously renounced my book and offered my children, completely, a parent. I had to do the former to allow the latter. These were the same act after all. I had to let the core of me die—for a while, at least—that they might properly live.

Ah, Mother, every summer since then I have thought of you and of all your sisters through the ages. I see you, darling, distinctly—as in a vision. I see deep, and I see this: that once there lay in the precinct of many mothers' souls some precious personal thing. Some talent, some private dream. The characteristic by which they defined their *selves* and their purpose for being. To write? Maybe. To run a marathon? Or to run a company? Yes. Yes.

But then the baby came home, and then you and others like you made a terrible, terribly lovely choice. You reached into your soul and withdrew that precious thing and lifted it up before your breast and began to walk. Deliberate and utterly beautiful, you strode to an altar of love for this child and placed there the talent, the dream, some core part of your particular *self*—and in order to mother another, you released it. There came for you a moment of conscious, sacred sacrifice. In that moment the self of yourself became a smoke, and the smoke went up to heaven as perpetual prayer for the sake of your children.

And when it was voluntary, it was no less than divine. Never, never let anyone force such a gift from any woman!—for then it is not sacrifice at all. It is oppression.

But never, either, dear children, take such an extraordinary love for granted. It is holy. For this, in the face of such women, is the mind of Christ, who emptied himself for us. And then again, for us.

Ah, Mother, I am so slow to know, but now I know—and out of the knowledge wherewith my own children have burdened me I thank you. From an overflowing heart, I thank you, Mother, for your motherhood.

COMMENCEMENT

OUTSIDE MY STUDY WINDOW, just this side of Bayard Park, sit two boys on the hood of a cream Camaro—in the process of becoming men.

How old are they? Well, their backs are to me. I see an occasional profile: sweet, smooth cheeks on the one boy, an innocent twinkle in his eye, rather chubby. The other is leaner, with broad, capable shoulders and a low brow. Athletic, obviously. God has given him a quality body. But how old? Seventeen? Eighteen at the most. Boys.

But they're speeding toward manhood with grave purpose.

And I grieve at the process. I am sick at heart for the men they wish to become and the means whereby they intend to achieve it.

Jekyll drank something, and Hyde sprang forth. These, too, begin by drinking—although their ritual is much more elaborate and clearly rehearsed. It smacks of tradition. It's been handed down to them. And watch! In thirty minutes they shall be men. Men after the image of . . . someone. There is some model in their minds according to which they are shaping themselves.

Men.

Okay, so lean child hands chubby child a pint, the flat bottle shrewdly concealed in brown paper. They exchange a bolder bottle of orange juice. They suck. They stare across the park, unspeaking yet. They are thinking great thoughts, obviously. They are, at this point, discovering that they have as much right to think great thoughts as any president of the United States, and the capacity, too. Or else they are merely waiting for the warm transformation of their minds so that the great thoughts already thought, already lodged above, might be released and descend. They suck. A car drives by. The bottles slide down between their thighs, but neither child ceases his stare. This is a solemn moment. They suck.

A little conversation now begins between them. I can't hear it; but by the nodding and the pursing of lips, I know: they consider their words to be uttered in wisdom; and they are in agreement together, lean kid and large kid. The great thoughts are coming down, now, like a sober rain. Manhood is arising. It is not just that they are beginning to feel good, but that they are feeling good *about themselves,* in every respect children of this progressive world. Aye, the smiling world should be proud of two who learn so well. Moreover, each of these feels he's in fine company.

It's time for the second agent of their maturation.

While lean fellow stretches his marvelous spine, hunches his athletic shoulders, and rolls his neck (gazing forever across the park), chunky fellow produces a Ziploc plastic bag. The shreds of dried vegetation inside are most carefully shaken onto white paper, the which is balanced on a finger, licked, rolled, and twisted at the ends. Sealed. Skillfully shapen and sealed. I am impressed by the earnest attention to ceremony given this act. There's more than mere practicality in chubby child's gestures; there is symbol and meaning and obedience, as if he were priesting at an altar and handling sacred elements. There is, clearly, a "right way" to roll a roach. And he who does it "right" is an initiate. He's passed some test. He is a man.

The white twist, now, is lit with fire. It burns. The round cheese-chunk of a fellow sucks on it. Then, with sacramental care—not looking at his brother, keeping his own face passive, gazing across the park—he passes it to the bean beside him, who performs the same rite: sucking. They are sharing.

Conversation develops a new weight. It becomes louder.

Lean kid slips from the hood of the Camaro. He begins to wave his arms, to stab the air with a pointed forefinger, to snap his head back at particularly critical strokes of rhetoric.

Lean kid is preaching.

Great thoughts, thoughts first conceived in an alcoholic fume then passed from mind to mind in devout conversation, thoughts consecrated by Mary Jane's numb benediction, these thoughts have now become *opinions*. Lean boy has opinions. He has, by the flash of his eye and the crack of his delivery, judgments to pass on many things within the world. Clearly, he feels he has a calling and the right to make them. Even so, he is above the world he criticizes. Even so, he has arrived. He is a man.

See him strut and frown? He's a passionate fellow. Do you see him beat his chest? Lo: *he* is the sweeter substance of all his thought. He has elevated *himself* by the elevation of his mind. There is no doubt, now: he can do great deeds. And do you see how he receives the approval of his brother, who roars and thumps the hood of the Camaro? He is not only wise, he is right! Hear him shout, despite the glances of more conventional passersby. Not only right: yo!— he is free.

Lean baby and chubby baby, they are men now. They possess a certain swelling self-importance. They've found their places in the universe.

And I grieve.

Where are the other men, the men who served as models for this travesty? Where are the true adults—by years, adults—who considered their lifestyles to be their "own business" and did not notice younger, watchful, malleable eyes desiring to make it *their* business, too? Where are these heroes and teachers of the children, these failures in plain responsibility, these liars of the good life, these fathers, older brothers, uncles, friends? Frauds! Around their necks should be hung the millstone Jesus described. Carve in that millstone the epitaph, *Just doin' my own thing. Ain't hurtin' no one.* Then cast them into the depths of the sea for having tempted little ones to sin.

Little children, strutting men!

God help them all.

In the end these two step away from their Camaro and perform a final rite of virility. They reverence the tree.

Lean fool and chubby fool stand side by side in silence, facing the trunk of a huge oak, their legs spread, their hands hidden below, their heads bowed down, peeing.

Then they zip. And then they drive the Camaro away to confront their destiny somewhere in the humdrum traffic.

P.U.T.T.T.

I DON'T WANT CEREAL on my kitchen floor. Does anyone? Is there anywhere a rational person who is not distressed by cereal on the kitchen floor?

Well, it grinds the no-wax floor I've just no-waxed. It murders the shine and my good mood. At night it hectors my sleep with dreams of a house buried in Cheerios. In the morning it sticks to my socks. It blackens dried dribbles of orange juice.

So what? So am I a lunatic to ask my children not to spill cereal on the kitchen floor? Is this a law too difficult to bear? No, this is basic and reasonable cleanliness.

It's unarguably healthy.

Then why, when hopping on one foot and declaring myself unhappy about cereal on the kitchen floor, do my children gape at me as if I'm countermanding some previous command that they *should* spill cereal on the floor, together with milk and a little orange juice? Why do they indicate my insanity then? And why do their wounded eyes call me the only warden in the world upset by a little cereal?

O fathers and mothers of the world, unite!

And what about homework? Does my daughter do her homework to benefit *me*? Am I enlightened by her learning? Will my name appear on the report card? Will I get a job thereby? Well, of course not. I am myself not a whit improved by her endeavor.

But then why, when I require of her the work that shall reward none but her, does she groan? Why does she pout and glower at me as if I've just ruined her life for my own satisfaction? I HATE GLOWERING!

Why do my children, in the best of moods, humor me—and; in the worst, act punished, imprisoned, unjustly troubled by a mindless giant?

Yours too?

O parents, unite!

My second son, whose back ripples with quick strength on a basketball court, is suddenly crippled by the mere mention of the lawn mower. It is his job to walk the dog. He has never walked a dog in his life, poor troubled soul.

And I have considered the regular series of emotions that cripple *me* when that same son is late for his curfew:

1. Mild annoyance (the kid is snitching minutes, though he promised to be home on time);

2. Anger, hotter by the hour;

3. Earnest worry, laced with guilt (is he hurt?—why did I blame the innocent child?);

4. And finally, crashing rage at his return and the explanation he offers, words meant to calm me by their reasoned and weighty consideration: "Uh, I forgot."

Every night, Matthew?

And can anyone explain to my own mother's son how it is that the lack of clean clothes is my fault?—when the cracker-jack kid neglected to throw her dirty clothes into the laundry?

Is it written somewhere that children must dress slowly, making everyone late for important occasions? Late and angry? I HATE TO BE LATE!

And who said that my cologne (and my socks and my razor and my room and my car and my wife's whole wardrobe) is theirs just because they inhabit the same house with us?

And did you know that TV is a teenager's constitutional right? Actually, noise is the right—any sort of noise: booming, strumming, shrieking, giggling.

And did you know that teenagers regularly detonate clothes-bombs in their bedrooms? The quicker the mess, the gladder the kid.

What do they do with our money anyway? Eat it?

O parents, one and all, what manner of thing have we sheltered all these years? What have we taken to our soft bosoms, which sprouted thereafter a vulture's beak and a taste for the flesh of progenitors? Teenagers! A breed apart.

It's a relatively new creature, this teen. For most of the world's history teenagers didn't exist. Until the last few hundred years, children ceased dependence upon their parents at fourteen, fifteen, sixteen, then shouldered their own apprenticeships, their labors and land and families. That wasn't considered too tender an age then; it certainly is no tender age today, but rough-cut and ready and stronger than I!

Parents, I have two proposals to make:

1. That once again we abolish teenagerhood; offer our fourteen-year-olds all rights of maturity, all the freedoms, and therewith all the responsibilities as well; throw them a *true* come-out party and give them luggage as a gift and mean it. If such a ritual of transition is universally observed, it'll benefit the nation whole. Think how much energy would be converted to solid work and taxable income—the which is now spent in malls on walking, talking, preening only. Think how we might augment the military, allay the national debt, and regain our place as first among industrial countries. Think of one father who will sleep unhectored by dreams of cereal on his kitchen floor.

Or, if my first proposal proves impossible, consider my second:

2. P.U.T.T. An organization entitled *Parents United To Tolerate Teenagers*.

Teenagerhood is, in fact, the kid's leave-taking from the family—extended over a longer period than in generations before. It is a normal process after all—a time when she learns independence and practices it, even while she is yet physically dependent upon her parents; a time of strife, then, and of inherent contradiction, but not of anything sick or sinful or wrong. The tension between independence and dependence causes violent shifts in attitudes. It confuses parent and child alike. The rules of relationship change daily; so what is a parent to *be* from Sunday to Tuesday?—A companion? A confidant? A cop? A teacher? Zoo keeper? Cheerleader? God?

Precisely during this period, dear parents, unite.

The process of separation is good and necessary, already defined in Genesis chapter two: *Therefore shall a man LEAVE his father and his mother, and shall CLEAVE unto his wife: and they shall be one flesh.* For any proper cleaving hereafter, there must be a true leaving now. The irritation, then, the pain of separation, the emotion and the provocation, the trouble and the break itself cannot be abolished, and it should not be avoided. It will be. Teens will bug us. And we them.

But we, their parents, might regularly support one another. Let's find stability with those who have managed (or who are managing) similar challenges, rather than demanding stability from the teens who, by the nature of their present passage, are as unstable as water. They simply cannot give it now.

Parents, let us laugh together by telling tales of the idiocy of these tall children. Laughter diminishes problems by granting a blessed release and a realistic perspective. Let's talk seriously, too; exchange advice; discover how very common, after all, is all that we thought bedeviled our family alone. And let's pray out loud. For each child by name. And for the parents. Because God is God of teenagers too. God is the one parent who shall *not* be superseded. And God will work internally in the confusing kid, using ways we can't even see.

For now we must love at a distance; but God never departs the intimate heart of the child. Never.

Ah, parents, attend to your own consolations now when the job of parenting *is* a job, an assignment, not a pleasure—and you will become a consolation for the teen who is as bewildered as yourself.

TO THE POOLS OF SILOAM

IT'S BEEN TWO SEASONS now since I saw her, but because of the tremendous respect she inspired in me (and then, as well, the pity) I can't forget her.

It picks at the back of my mind, over and over again, asking: *What does she remind me of?*

Something remarkable.

Last spring a duck entered our backyard journeying eastward, eleven little ducklings in file behind her. It was an outrageous appearing, really, since we live in the midst of the concrete city. The only waters east of us are the pools at the state hospital, four miles away, which distance is an odyssey! Between here and there are vast tracts of humanity, fences, houses, shopping malls—and immediately to our east, Bayard Park of tall trees and lawns.

Yet this duck moved her brood with a quick skill as if she knew exactly where she was going.

Buff brown generally, vague markings on her wings, a smooth pate with a cowlick at the back, she and her name were the same: blunt and unremarkable. The ducklings were puffballs with butch haircuts, obedient and happy. Big-footed, web-footed, monstrous-footed, floppy-footed, the children followed their mother as fast as drips down windowpanes, peeping, questioning, keeping together, trusting her judgment.

And she, both blunt and busy, led them into our yard, which is surrounded by a wooden palisade fence. Maybe she came this way for a rest.

But we have a dog. He rose to his feet at the astonishing sight. He raised his ears and woofed. The duck backpedaled to the wall of the house and turned eastward under the eaves' protection and waddled hard, her ducklings in mad zip behind her. But the dog is leashed and could not reach the wall. This part of the passage, at least, was safe. The next was not.

Without pausing, the buff duck spread her wings, beat the air, and barely cleared the fence, landing in the middle of Bedford Avenue between our yard and the park. There she set up a loud quacking, like a reedy woodwind: *Come! Come!*

Eleven ducklings scurried to the fence, then raced along it till they found a crack: *Plip! Plip!*—they popped through as quick as they could, but their mother must have been driven into the park. By the time they gained the wider world she had disappeared. The babies bunched in confusion, peeping, peeping grievously. One bold soul ventured down Bedford to the alley behind our yard. The others returned through the fence.

Immediately the mother was back on Bedford, the one bold child behind her, scolding the rest like an angry clarinet: *Now! Here! Come here now!*

Well, in a grateful panic ten ducklings rushed the crack in the fence, thickening there, pushing, burning with urgency, trying hard to obey their mother—

Not fast enough.

A car roared south on Bedford. Another. The duck beat retreat to the farther curb. Joggers came jogging. A knot of teenagers noticed the pretty flow of ducklings from under our fence and ran toward it. The tiny flock exploded in several directions. The mother's cries grew hectic and terrified: *Come! Come!*—her beak locked open. She raced up and down the park's edge, and there was but the one puffball following her.

The simple unity of twelve was torn apart. My city is deadly to certain kinds of families.

Five ducklings shot back and forth inside our yard now, but the hole through the fence led to roaring horrors and they couldn't persuade themselves to hazard it again—though they could hear their mother. That unremarkable duck (no!—intrepid now and most remarkable) was hurling herself in three directions, trying to compose her family in unity again: eastward she flew into the park, south toward violent alleys, then back west to the impassive fence. *Hear me now, hear me and come!* Her children were scattered. She was but one.

I saw a teenager chase one duckling. He was laughing gaily in the game. He reached down and scooped up the tiny life in his great hand and peered at it and then threw it up into the air. The baby fell crazily to the ground. The youth chased it again.

"Don't!" I yelled.

"Why not?" the kid said, straightening himself. "What? Does this duck belong to you?"

But where was the mother now? I didn't see her anywhere. And now it was bending into the later afternoon.

I poured some water into a pan and placed it by the back wall of the house for those ducklings still dithering within our yard. They huddled away from the dog. But the dog had lost interest. They crept sometimes toward the hole in the fence. Now and again a duckling looked through. Their peeping, peeping was miserable. What do you do for innocents in the city—both the wild and the child? By nightfall they had all vanished.

No, not all. I can tell you of two.

The next day we heard a scratching in the vent pipe of our clothes dryer. I went down in the basement and disconnected the shaft and found a shivering duckling who must have fallen down from the outside opening. Perhaps it had sought cover and didn't know the cave went down so deep. It had spent a long dark night alone in its prison.

And then at church on Sunday a friend of mine said, "Weirdest thing! I saw this duck crossing highway 41—"

"What?" I cried. "A duck? Alone?"

"Well, no, not alone," said my friend. "I almost ran over her. I guess she didn't fly on account of baby ducks can't fly, and she was protecting it."

"Michelle," I said, "what do you mean *it*? How many ducklings did she have?"

"One. Just one."

There have passed two seasons, I say, since I encountered this blunt, buff duck—and still in my heart I whisper as I did then, *Godspeed* with honor and pity. *Godspeed, remarkable creature, tenacious and loving.*

And now I know what she reminds me of.

Of single-parent families in a largely indifferent world.

She reminds me of that impoverished mother (Oh, my culpable country!) who has small means to nourish and raise and protect her children. I have met that mother far too often with far too little to offer her. Mighty is her love. Illogical, absurd, and marvelous is her love for the children. And terrible is her sorrow for the loss of any one of them. The world may not enlarge her love or else diminish her sorrow. The world may in fact begrudge whatever little thing it gives her. Worse: the world can be dangerous to the family whole and to her children in particular.

But she loves. This mother knows from the beginning that the children will be chased, harassed, scorned, beaten, belittled—both by raggedy folks and by the upright and civil people of her city. She knows that one child may tumble down black shafts of a blatant disregard and another into drugs and another into crime and another into despair. From the beginning their prospects must wring her heart with a tight anxiety. She labors to give them a life for a while and some esteem and safety—and against desperate odds, marvelously, she loves.

To this one I say, *Godspeed, good parent, all the way east to the pools of Siloam and your children's maturity.*

And to the holy community of the church I say: *Help her! Surround this single parent, mother or father, with love and a service equal to her own. No: with a love equal to God's, whom you are sent to represent!*

In God's name, help her.

"I ALWAYS KNEW
YOU'D CALL"

i.

My daughter's father's name is Carter.

Until Talitha was in college, I didn't know his name. Well, I didn't know the man. I knew only that some such person must exist. Because my daughter existed.

Often when we sat at supper, I would look across the table at Talitha and seek in her features the faces of her begetters. They seemed always to hover ghostly behind her, their faces indistinct, blurred versions of her own face. Her father, I knew, was African American, her mother white. And because Talitha, who has been our daughter since the eighth month of her life, was growing older among us, so were the presences of these two anonymous souls.

But they were the blank part, the root of this child still deep down in the soil. Talitha's birth parents had made her in their image, and I sought those images in her: a slant, receding jaw, softly curling hair, high cheeks, an aggressive personality. Would I recognize either one if I met the mother or the father on the street? How much is our daughter *ours*, after all, and how much theirs?

The man and the woman were ghosts in the family, not because they were not, but because they were not known.

Now Joseph was a righteous man. He obeyed the word of God, whether written in the laws of Moses or else uttered in dreams by angels. He obeyed, and obedience made a marriage where there

167

might have been divorce. Obedience saved his son from Herod's hatred. Joseph's obedience took him to Egypt and then again to the security of Nazareth, where it shaped the daily life of his family by offerings and sacrifices and the keeping of feasts.

The more I think of this man in whom meekness was a strength, the more I honor him. Unlike Zechariah—who mistrusted the word of God—Joseph was not made mute. Yet the Bible records no word spoken by Joseph. Most folks involved in the events of the Nativity talked. They sang and chattered and expostulated. Everyone! Kings, priests, scribes, relatives, neighbors. Even the shepherds. But not Joseph. He didn't talk. He obeyed. Silently and steadfastly his word was ever his deed. He acted. He served.

Yet the man was no one's puppet. And his heart was kind. Joseph chose to temper righteousness with tenderness. Whether the law accused her or not, he would never put Mary to shame. Nor would he leave her behind when he, as head of the household, went to the City of David to be enrolled. He might have. He could have. Most husbands would have left the matter of childbirth behind them, at home, in the hands of women, since this was women's business, surely.

But Joseph took Mary with him. And in Bethlehem a babe was born which was not his own, even as he knew beforehand that it would not be. In the face of this infant he would never find his older face reflected. Nevertheless, kindly, righteously, Joseph adopted the child.

Perhaps you are already aware that Joseph is the patron saint of the fathers of families. I think he stands as a model for all parents, in fact, because the ghostly unknown that hovered behind his adopted son—the Begetter of *this* boy, in whose features was the First Father's image—is also the Primal Parent of every child ever born in the world. And God's heavenly parenthood makes all mothers and all fathers the adopters of their children.

But I feel a particular friendship for Joseph. Our fatherhoods are so similar that I cannot but learn from his plain response to the glorious task of raising the Son of Another: his faith, his obedience, his tenderness—and finally his willing release of the child. The child was his but a little while. . . .

~

ii.

In May 1993 Thanne and I were driving Talitha back home from college. We had just passed through Louisville on Interstate 65 and were crossing the Ohio River into Indiana when Talitha leaned forward from the back seat, held her face between our faces a moment, gazing at the road ahead, then spoke.

The van was full to the roof with of her stuff, so the rear view mirror was blocked by boxes—and now by my daughter's earnest brow. I recall how like logs the ladder-like shadows of the bridge's top-structure fell across the windshield in quick rhythm: *Poom, poom, poom, poom—*

Thanne had begun to turn her attention toward Talitha, opening her mouth around some pleasant word, when the girl abruptly declared: "I want to stop in Frankfort."

That declaration has fixed the moment in my memory forever.

I glanced at her in the mirror. She was not looking at us. I returned my gaze to the road, saying, "Really? Are you sure?"

Frankfort is a small town about thirty-five miles northwest of Indianapolis. For all the years we'd lived in this state, both south and north of little Frankfort, we had never stopped there before. We had, of course, known its name. For us the name had borne a peculiar significance. In me a certain emotion attended the speaking of it, because we had her birth records, and we knew: this is the place where Talitha was born, nineteen years ago.

She said, "Are you challenging me?"

I was about to say, *No, of course not.*

But Thanne spoke to me directly: "Yes, she's sure."

I glanced at both women.

"What?" I said. "Have you two been discussing something without me?"

Thanne said, "Wally."

I frowned.

Again, urging me to look at her, Thanne said, "Wally."

And when I did glance at her, with emphasis she said, "No. We have not been talking."

I said nothing then, but entered a private bewilderment and continued to drive north. Frankfort was still more than a hundred and forty miles away.

Two days earlier Talitha Michal Wangerin had finished the final exams of her first year at Spelman. This is a historically Black women's college, an excellent institution, free in the faith—and God's merciful answer to prayers her mother had been praying for Talitha's salvation and her safety.

My child! My daughter in high school had been grimly rebellious—almost as though rebellion were the job of the proper teenager. Talitha is and ever will be a fighter, a swashbuckler: fearless, willful and willing to fight for her rights as she perceives them. It's a marvelous, martial collection of characteristics; but lacking maturity, it had also lacked the wisdom to distinguish which rights were worth the fight, which were merely whimsical, and which were plain selfish. Thus the drama and the trauma of her adolescence.

Thanne went toe to toe with the girl. If Talitha screamed, my gentle wife screamed back, word for word and hoot for hoot. I knew even then it was the parent's job that Thanne was herself accomplishing. And it produced in her daughter astonishment early and her admiration late. But this particular display of parental love took my breath away. Mute before a screaming match, fearing I might hit something or someone, I would hurl myself bodily into the dark nights to walk long and lonely and far away, considering the talents of these two women against my perfect helplessness.

Actually, I stood in awe of this youngest of our children on many counts: she could schedule herself to the fractions of a minute, studying, playing, eating and *sleeping* according to her own clock. Talitha did conscientiously shape herself into a student! She was willing to "try out" for everything, expected to fail at some things in order to find her aptitude for a few. She chose independence. Independence was for my daughter a religion. Woe, therefore! Woe to anyone, sister or father, who woke the girl from sleep earlier than her schedule had planned for waking. Why, she came up from her cave like a she-bear, claws extended.

Well, so Thanne and I watched while state schools offered Talitha scholarships, watched and prayed that somehow she would choose Spelman, watched and prayed and *never* argued for Spelman (because her independence would on principle reject such parental persuasions), watched and praised the dear Lord God when she, choosing Black—choosing to *be* Black—chose Spelman.

Approaching the south side of Indianapolis I formed and I asked the question that would at least entitle Tabitha's present determinations.

"Why," I said, "do you want to stop in Frankfort?"

And she said, "I want to find my birth parents."

Yes. Yes, that had been my own wordless assumption. But at the speaking of the matter, things felt suddenly and vastly reversed: all at once I, the adoptive father, had become the ghost; *my* father-hood was the fatherhood invisible. For my daughter had begun to peer through me, seeking the features of her begetters. And though I may have been a tool, a means to that end, theirs—those primary beings, flesh-and-blood at her conceiving—was the substance Talitha desired. In *them*, now, she sought her identity and her self.

What should I do in the next fifty miles? What word should I obey, now? Tabitha's? Or that different word which hovered behind my lips as I slowed for Indianapolis?

Or else some deeper murmurings of Almighty God?

Such a moment, I believe, also occurred for Joseph.

Jesus never challenged his adoptive father's authority the way Talitha did ours. Luke says he "was obedient to" his parents. Yet, there were intimacies in which this father could not participate. For he likely would sit at a Passover meal and look into his son's face and find there absolutely no characteristic of his own.

Mary's eyes, perhaps, the curve of *her* jaw. He could see a mother-son relationship, but he could only watch. It was a parenthood beyond his reach.

Someone else dwelt in his son's face. Another source governed the boy's behavior. Indistinct, completely different, strange to Joseph, a ghost in the household.

Training up the child of one's own loins has a deep spiritual and genetic appropriateness. One doesn't question one's right and the instinctive rightness of one's methods. Communication is as deep as the chromosomes. Thanne and I have raised children born to us as well as children adopted, and we've experienced the difference. Unto one's born children, for example, a raised eyebrow can speak powerfully, because they *feel* the command in the lift of their own eyebrow and, internally, in the sense of such a gesture. External behavior speaks to internal emotion, when the speakers share the both together.

On the other hand, in order to train up the adopted child, one must also learn *her* language, since communication needs must begin at the surface of things. One must never assume a complete knowledge of this child—except as watchfulness reveals her to the hungry love of her parents. And very early the adoptive parent realizes that the methods of training *this* child must obey a greater source than flesh and natural conception.

I'm speaking for Joseph, as well as for myself. He must have trained Jesus with a more conscious loving, a more patient searching of his son in order to learn the character of the stranger placed into his care. And I am convinced that Joseph founded his right to raise this child upon the word of God—the immediate message of the angels, and the covenantal law, the righteousness required of all faithful fathers. Joseph sought the source of his authority in God, and he accomplished it by obedience to God and by faith.

In the regular day-to-day labor of raising children (all our children, those adopted in the flesh *and* those adopted in the spirit), Thanne and I have stood in the shadow of this common, quiet man.

But then comes the frightening moment, the vast reversal when present parenthood grows ghostly and invisible because the child is seeking his identity in Another. . . .

Joseph and Mary and Jesus took a trip. The little family traveled from Nazareth to Jerusalem. All was well. They went to celebrate the Passover, and since Jesus was twelve—an age of transitions not unlike the eighteenth year of our children today—this may have been his first experience of the feast. This was the year when the Law required his father to acquaint him with the duties and regulations that he would assume as a thirteen-year-old male.

So Joseph did what was required of him. He bought a lamb. He took Jesus to watch the priest's ritual slaughter of the lambs. He showed his boy the Temple itself. They went together through the Gates Beautiful into the court of the Israelites, where they stood less than fifteen meters from the High Altar itself. Joseph faithfully enacted parenthood, and then the little family began to travel home again.

Suddenly, late in the journey, the parents realized that their child was absent. He was nowhere among the pilgrims, and because their love was genuine, they rushed all the way back to Jerusalem in a panic.

When was it that Joseph suffered the prickly feeling that he was seeking a stranger? When did he admit that he didn't know his son well enough to guess where the lad would hang out in Jerusalem? They spent three days searching everywhere *except* in the temple. And when they found Jesus sitting there, they were, says Luke, "astonished" by his ability to amaze even the teachers: a stranger!

The boy's mother was upset. Mary took it personally: "Why have you done this to us?" she said. "Your father and I have been so worried, looking for you!"

As Luke records the scene, the adoptive father was quiet.

But then occurred the moment of vast reversals, when Joseph became the ghost past whom his son was peering to see his Real Father, in whose substance was his self.

"Why were you looking for me?" Jesus said. "Didn't you know that I must be in my Father's house?"

Let no one ever diminish the depth and the complexity of Joseph's response. It is right now that faith and obedience and mercy and a parent's personal choosing all had their most significant effect!

Joseph obeyed.

Whose word did he obey? No word nor wound in his own heart! Neither pride nor self-pity controlled him, for he continued as before—never changing—to be the father of this boy, taking him home again to Nazareth.

Joseph "did not understand the saying" that Jesus had spoken to him. Intellectually, the plain man was ignorant. Yet he acted nevertheless, because obedience is always possible—even, and especially, without knowledge! Joseph acted by obeying the words God had already spoken to him. And though he did not directly submit to the saying of his son (which would have given the child rule of his household), he did obey the deeper meaning behind the saying—for there it was that God dwelt.

Here, then, is the saint of parenthood and the model for Thanne and me: this father, not comprehending all that was going on around him, receiving the lesser respect of his own son—this adoptive father chose mercifully still to *be* a father. By faith! In obedience. Already now he ceased to covet his child's first love and praise and honor. The quiet man was also a humble man. In fact, he could best fulfill his parental role precisely because he did not do it for his own benefit.

Thus a plain man accomplished a task of terrible glory, raising a child who was born in the image of God. Has any parent a different task than that?

Luke writes that Jesus was "obedient" to Joseph and Mary thereafter. In their household he "increased in wisdom and in stature and in favor with God" and with the neighbors.

By loving God, Joseph loved Jesus rightly. And by following God, Joseph led his son out of the house, into adulthood and into the purpose for which he was born. A righteous father raised a righteous son, then released him finally to the righteousness of his greater ministry.

iii.

We stopped in Frankfort. We found the courthouse where birth records were kept, and the Lutheran Church where Talitha's birth mother might have attended, and the high school, and the hospital where our daughter was born.

The town was altogether white. It seemed to us that the presence of a Black man nineteen years ago might have caused a stir. Perhaps it might be remembered by someone.

And because Talitha's first mother had kept her for eight months before giving the baby up for adoption, we believed that the birth had not been a secret. We also felt that those eight months must have made the infant dear to the young mother. These things persuaded Thanne and me to agree with our daughter's desires and not to discourage them.

We chose Joseph's way: to parent in humility, allowing our child a self-discovery which must take her beyond our own spheres and influence, yet continuing to parent her even during the search, and forever praying her Heavenly Father's benevolence upon her.

Be born, Talitha. Be born a second time, this time into a knowing and a heritage and an identity.

Obeying the Lord, who gives us children for a little while before they must enter their independent lives and purposes completely, we chose to help her seek her source. If things grew destructive, we would be there. If things developed unto goodness, we would stand by, watching. But if we had denied her this choice in the first place, we'd have canceled not her looking but ourselves, and would ourselves have missed everything thereafter, whether troubled or glorious.

So our sassy, pushy daughter returned to Frankfort that summer. And Thanne's spirit more than mine hovered over her entire adventure. Of course it did: she told me that she had, during the last several years, been expecting Talitha to initiate this search. For once they had been watching an Oprah Winfrey show wherein birth parents met their children for the first time. Talitha got up and went into the bathroom, Thanne said. When she came out again, Thanne saw that she had been crying. It was a clue.

"So," Talitha said, standing in the secretary's office at the high school, "do you remember a Black man about town nineteen years ago? Did he have a baby by a woman here?"

She and Thanne talked with administrators of the county, of the hospital, of the newspaper. They kept notes. One or two people remembered details of the past. By midsummer they had nosed the family name of the woman who had brought Talitha to birth.

And then they learned the woman's first name. Mary.

The old ghosts were growing evermore present. And I was feeling evermore ghostly. I wondered: the closer Talitha came to *that* mother and father, would she travel farther and farther from us?

But, in ignorance and in humility, faithfully, we parents obey. We seek the wholeness of our children as God conceived that wholeness from the beginning. We hunt their identities in the past, in order to uncover their purposes for the future. Clinging can kill these things, surely!

Early in September, after Talitha had returned to Spelman, she and Thanne finally learned the first name of Mary's father, and that he still lived in Frankfort! He was their link. They discussed how best to approach him and to ask the address and the telephone number of his daughter.

How much could be gained! How much could be lost in this single telephone call.

"You do it," Talitha said. "I can't."

Thanne agreed. But she swallowed hard before the doing. And she prayed and she trembled. She told me that she absolutely would not lie. How could she seek truth by false means? Yes, but if she misspoke her request, if she suddenly raked up old odors and emotions, the man might well hang up, and the link would break.

She dialed Frankfort from our home in Valparaiso.

A woman answered.

Thanne asked for Mary's father by name.

When he came on the line, Thanne said, "My daughter knew your daughter years ago. But she has lost contact. Can you give me her phone number and address?"

There was a distinct hesitation at the other end of the line. Then the man said, "Wait." He returned. Slowly he gave Thanne the information, and he hung up without a question.

Immediately Thanne called Talitha.

"She lives in Dallas, Texas," Thanne said, panting.

And then she hung up. But she stayed by the phone, scarcely moving. Talitha was, as that same moment, dialing the number in Dallas. Such union in these women's hearts and goals! This adoptive mother dwelt in the terrible excitement of her daughter as the younger one sought to talk with another mother completely.

The phone rang.

Thanne snatched it up.

Ah, but a mother almost weeps with her daughter's disappointment. She and Talitha spoke softly a while, and then went each to her own business. The number in Dallas had been disconnected, and they were at a dead end.

It is precisely here that I believe her Supernal Parent to have intervened. God the Father joined the search. For Talitha took a trip to Evansville. There she visited friends. Among the people she stopped to see was a family in our old neighborhood, where she used to baby sit. On their tea table was a copy of the Frankfort High School yearbook.

"Did you," she asked the husband, "go to that high school?"

"Yes," he said. Ach! And they had known each other for so many years!

Talitha asked, "Did you know a Mary W____?"

"Only by name," he said. "She was several classes behind. Wait— but they had a reunion last year, and I know who has a list of names and addresses. . . ."

This man obtained that list. And Mary W____'s telephone number, still in Dallas. He passed the information to Talitha, now back in Atlanta.

Late that same night, Talitha called Thanne, screaming, "I have it! I have it! I know Mary's telephone number—"

Thanne didn't scream. She became the voice of reason: "Talitha, it's late. Don't call her tonight. You know how much *you* hate it when someone wakes you up."

That night neither Thanne nor Talitha slept. Restless, restless, the ghost was taking flesh. The ghost was *there*, waiting for the telephone to ring.

By seven in the morning, Atlanta time, Talitha could wait no longer.

She dialed the number. She heard the pulse of the ring in Dallas.

Then the connection was made. A woman's voice came over the lines: "Hello? What?"

Talitha tells me that she had planned to ask just two questions, and then to make a statement.

She said, "Is this Mary W--?"

The woman said, "Yes."

And then Talitha asked, "Did you have a baby girl on January ninth, nineteen-seventy-four?"

There was a breathing pause. Finally the woman said, "Yes. I did."

Talitha made her statement: "I have reason to believe," she said, "that I am the baby that you had."

Now there stretched between Dallas and Atlanta a silence too weighty and too long. But Talitha did not hang up. Finally she spoke into the silence, saying, "I can call you back later."

And the woman answered.

Mary W_____ said, "I always knew you would call—[pause]—I just didn't think you'd call at six and WAKE ME UP!"

My daughter's father's name is Carter. He is very short and very dark. He lives in North Carolina. So does his mother, our daughter's grandmother, Trula.

After Talitha had taken a trip from Atlanta to her house, Trula called Thanne. The elder woman was in tears.

"The baby called me Grandma!" she said to Thanne. "The baby called me Grandma."

This woman had been praying for that "baby," she said, ever since the child had been swallowed into the darkness of adoption.

And we have visited with the Frankfort side of Talitha's family. Her white birth grandfather knocked tears out of his eyes when he met her for the first time. "You are a part of us," he said with a rough-hewn formality.

Sitting in his living room, he looked at Thanne. "You called me up, didn't you."

She admitted it.

He said, "I knew this call was different. It was her." He pointed at his wife. "She reckoned the difference too. She pushed me. She said to give you the number."

And we have met Mary _____, whom we now call "Mother Mary" to distinguish her from our daughter, Talitha's "Sister Mary."

The ghost has flesh! She is no longer ghostly. And I was not wrong all those years to seek the face of the begetter in the child's face. Mary has precisely the same slant to her jaw, the same high cheekbones, the same aggressive character. They laugh alike, talk alike, aggress alike, bear their bodies quite alike, since the bodies, too, reflect each other. They are good friends, now. And Talitha has learned both her own infant history and the histories of her families. She hath a bloodline and a heritage!

But neither have Thanne and I been rendered invisible. We are flesh and blood, still, and parents of our child.

Simply: we, too, see her face in the faces of *all* her parents: Mary and Carter and the Almighty, dear and loving Creator God who stands behind all and collects all in his everlasting union.

The ghost in Jesus was holy. In him all the fullness of God was pleased to dwell. This is what Joseph by his plain, faithful obedience was granted to see: Immanuel, God with us.

In all our children's faces is the image of their Creator. When parents, by loving God, love their children right; and when, by following God, parents lead their children out of the house, into adulthood and into the purposes for which they were born, then in the fullness of their grown children they, too, will find the face of God the Father—who had lent them the children in the first place. And for a little while.

Gently, gently, parents, stand aside, even as a grandmother named Trula once stood so long aside and did her duty by praying.

After the nativity stories, Joseph's name appears again, on the lips of those who are trying to place the identity of this Jesus from

Nazareth. But the man himself finally decreases almost completely, as his adopted son increases, and the greater Father is glorified by the increase.

iv.

In those days we learned that Talitha's birth name had been Cassindra Marie. It was for "Cassindra Marie" that Trula had prayed on every holiday and on every ninth day of January, trusting her to the care of the Father.

("And see?" Trula said to us while we sat beneath Stone Mountain, celebrating our child's graduation from Spelman. "See? God heard every one of my prayers! You," she said, looking significantly at Thanne and me, "you were God's answerings all along.")

"Cassindra Marie." Talitha cherished the name as a living contact both to who she was in the beginning and to those who nursed her then.

And now our daughter has children of her own, grandchildren in triumph unto these aging adoptive parents, Ruthanne and I.

But here's a circle so cosmic it is beyond my own poor comprehension: that Talitha named her firstborn daughter by the name first empties and now made full again:

Her daughter's name, our granddaughter's name, is Cassindra Marie.

KEEPSAKE

Oh, my children! What can I bequeath
You more than stories? Lips don't last: they dry
Soon, tremble soon, and die; but that they breathed
Warm words against your hair and kissed your eyes—
That will remain in memory a story.
All of the goods I leave you you will use
Up, digging out the goodness as they quarry
Carrara: I can't stay in what you choose
To change—and you *will* choose when I cannot.
But stories deep as fairy tales, as searching
As poetry, as hoary, unforgot
And vulvar as the *Heilsgeschichte*, cursing
And blessing at once—these stand mining (whether
I'm dead, ye delvers, or alive) forever.

THE PARENT OF HIS PARENTS

LIVE LONG ON THE EARTH

THE COMMANDMENTS HAVE NOT expired. Nor have the holy promises that attend them been abolished.

When, therefore, I am asked regarding the future of some human community, some family, some nation—or the church, the visible church itself!—straightway I look for obedience to the commandments of God. Particularly I wonder regarding the one which urges honor for the parents: I look to see whether someone is singing songs to his aged mother—and if I can find him, I say, "The signs are good."

This is no joke. The best prognostication for the life of any community—whether it shall be long or short—is not financial, political, demographic, or even theological. It is moral. Ask not, "How strong is this nation?" nor "How many are they? How well organized? With what armies and resources?" Ask, rather: *How does this people behave?*

See, there is always set before us life and good or death and evil. If we walk in the ways of the sustaining God and obey his commandments, then we have chosen life—for the Lord *is* life and the length of any nation's days. This is flat practicality. How we *are* defines whether we shall continue to *be*.

Do we as a people honor our mothers and our fathers? Do we honor the generation that raised us—especially when it sinks down into an old and seemingly dishonorable age? When our parents twist and bow and begin to stink, what then? When they harden in crankiness, what then? Do we by esteeming them make them sweet and lovely again? The question is not irrelevant to our future, whether we shall have one or not. Its answer verily prophesies of *That it may be well with you and you may live long on the earth.*

The Hebrew word here translated *earth* may also be translated *land,* meaning more than just soil, meaning *country.* The promise

185

attached to this commandment is precise: so long as the Israelites honored their parents, they would continue to live in the land that God had provided for them. If ever they began to neglect their parents or, worse, to scorn or in some way to hurt them, that break between the generations would break the people from their land as a sick tree breaks at the trunk and dies.

Even so we—as long as we sing to the mother who bore us the songs she heard in her youth, the same songs once she sang to us in lullaby—we may live long in the land.

I have seen the signs. In Wisconsin. In quiet obscurity, where I went to visit a friend of mine who lives with his mother in the farmhouse her father built one hundred years ago. She has a wasting disease. My friend cares for her.

M. is a studious man. In the evening he reads by a low lamp in the corner of the parlor. The light casts shadows on an ancient florid wallpaper, on heavy furniture, on the bed in the farther darkness where his mother sleeps. He reads through half-glasses, his head bent to the page, fingers at his chin. He reads very late because his mother may murmur softly—too softly to be heard from any other part of the house—and this is his signal to serve her.

But when he welcomed me to the farmhouse, it was daylight. He opened the door and grinned with thin lips his genuine pleasure at my coming and immediately invited me to the parlor.

The house smelled sweet and brown with cinnamon, tart with apples.

"Your mother's baking?" I asked as we walked.

"No," he said and ducked his head a bit, an angular apology. "No, she doesn't do that anymore."

"Then who—?"

"Oh, well," he said. Sheepish. "I see to the necessary things."

We entered the parlor, and so I understood.

His mother was sitting up in bed, a shawl around her shoulders, smiling. I, too, smiled and walked toward her. But M. interposed, introducing us with a formal civility as if the woman were very rich, as if we had never met before: "Mother, be pleased to meet—"

In fact, I've known M.'s mother almost as long as I have known him. But now it became clear that she had ceased to know me, and I was startled by the change. Her face was round, slack, soft, white, and, except for the querulous smile, expressionless. My dear old friend who once wore an apron and cooked for me, her face had the glaze of a dinner plate. Her watery glance never found my eyes but dribbled down my chest to my hands as if she were a child looking for candy.

M. said, "Shake hands with mother."

I did. As I reached, her right arm rose spontaneously. I took the powder-white hand that hung at the wrist and squeezed something like dough. She never ceased to smile, but questioningly. I stepped back. M. offered her a prune from a dish. She had a wonderful set of teeth. She was munching when we left the room.

We talked the rest of the day, M. and I. We strolled a sharp autumn countryside as the sun descended and the chill came down and the air smelled of crushable things, husks and hulls and leaves and the scented fires that burn them.

All the farmland had been sold, except five acres and the house itself. They kept a small orchard—and that was floating on the cool air too, a winey aroma.

I have always enjoyed the probing intellect of my friend's conversation: soft-spoken, forever undismayed, M. has a natural savvy which he has enriched with his reading. He could, if they would listen, counsel presidents.

Finally it was the night. I praised his apple pie and retired to my room and lay down and slept.

I tell you the truth—that very night I saw the signs:

At two in the morning I was awakened by a cry. I felt my stomach contract. I thought I heard a cat in the house, a lingering, feline wailing, inarticulate and mournful. It was a sort of screamed lamentation.

It seemed that someone was terribly hurt.

So I rose and followed the sound downstairs—through the kitchen to the parlor. A low lamp was lit. I peeped in.

This was no cat. This was M.'s mother. Her head was thrown backward, her mouth enormous, all her upper jaw and teeth in view. She was yowling: *Ya-ya-ya-na-naaaaah!*

M. himself was crouched at her bedside with a pan of water and cloths. He turned and saw me in the doorway. He smiled and motioned me to sit. I sat in his chair, under his reading lamp, granting them the privacy of darkness—but by the odor in the room I know what my friend was doing.

He was honoring his mother, exactly as the Lord God commanded.

He was washing away the waste. He was changing her diapers.

And he was singing to her.

Softly, in his mother's tongue, he was singing, *Müde bin ich, geh zu ruh*—Lullabies. The simple, sacred, everlasting songs.

And she was singing with him. That was the sound I had been hearing: no lamentation, no hurt nor sorrow, but an elderly woman singing with outrageous pleasure at the top of her lungs.

And lo: This old face was alive again. This old woman was as young as the child who first heard the lullaby, innocent, happy, wholly consoled. This old mother of my friend was dwelling in the music of her childhood. This was the face of one beloved, whose son obeyed the covenants and honored her—and kept her honorable thereby.

This boisterous singer is my sign. And the sign is good. Shall we endure? So long as such obedience continues among us, O my people, yes, it may be well with us. We may live long on the earth.

RED, RED, THE
BLOODRED KISS

TWO WEEKS AGO I sat in the crowded holding area at one of the gates of Houston's Intercontinental Airport, waiting to board my flight home. First dribblingly, and then wondrously in so public a place, laughter rose up by the door of the jetway. It became a loud, footstomping hoot.

I glanced up.

Two young women were rooting through the enormous purse of a third, an older bonier woman who was obviously nervous, obviously the traveler of the three.

"Where you *got* them Tums?" cried a younger woman, her face and her full right arm deep inside this purse. "You know you need— *Whoop!* " she shrieked. "Lookee here!"

Laughing, laughing till tears streamed from her eyes, she drew forth and held up five magazines, a sandwich wrapped in wax paper, earplugs, small cans of juice, an umbrella—and a new package of underwear entitled: *Three Briefs.*

"Mamma!" she cried. "Oh, Mamma, what you want with these?" The older woman looked baffled. The younger one laughed with a flashing affection. "You got plans you ain't tol' us about?" Maybe the two young women were daughters of their more solemn elder, maybe her granddaughters. "Honey, it's the Tums'll do you most good." She dived into the purse again. "Now where you got... Oh, Mamma. Oh, Mamma," she whispered with suddenly softer wonder: "Look."

This young woman had a magnificent expanse of hip and the freedom of spirit to cover it in a bright red skirt, tight at the waist, wide behind, and tight again at the knee. She stood on spiky heels. Fashion forced her to walk by short wobbly steps, oddly opposite her amplitude of hip and cheek and laughter.

"Oh, Mamma!" Suffused with gentleness, she pulled from the purse a worn leather-bound Testament and Psalms. "Mamma, what? What you thinkin'?" The two women exchanged a silent look, each full of the knowledge of the other. The generations did not divide them.

"Well," said the older, bony woman, "you found the nourishment, but you ain't found the Tums." With a bark of laughter, Young Woman in Red hunkered down into the purse again—tottering on her tiny heels.

At the same time there came down the concourse an old man so gaunt in his jaw as to be toothless, bald and blotched on his skull, meatless arm and thigh. He sat in a wheelchair, listing to the right. The chair was being pushed through the crowds at high speeds by an attendant utterly oblivious of this wispy, thin, and ancient passenger.

The old man's eyes were troubled, but his mouth, sucked inward, was mute. His nose gave him the appearance of a hawk caught in a trap, helpless and resigned.

Now the attendant turned into our gate area, jerked the chair to a stop (bouncing the skeletal soul therein), reached down to set the brake, turned on his heel, and left.

But the brake was not altogether set, nor had the chair altogether stopped. It was creeping by degrees toward the generous hips of the woman whose face was buried in the generous purse of her elder, giggling.

The old man's eyes—the closer he rolled to this red rear end as wide as Texas—widened. He opened his mouth. He began to raise a claw. He croaked. And then he ran straight into the back of her knees.

Yow! Up flew the great purse, vomiting contents. Backward stumbled the young woman, a great disaster descending upon a crushable old man.

At the last instant, she whirled around and caught herself upon the armrests of the wheelchair, a hand to each rest. Her face froze one inch from the face of an astonished octogenarian. They stared at one another, so suddenly and intimately close that they must have felt the heat—each must have smelled the odor of the other.

All at once the woman beamed. "Oh, honey!" she cried. "You somethin' handsome, ain't you?" She leaned the last inch forward and kissed him a noisy smack in the center of his bald head. "I didn't hurt you none, did I?"

Strangers were strangers no longer. Suddenly they were something more.

Slowly there spread over the features of this ghostly old man the most beatific smile. Oh, glory and heat and blood and love rose up in a body dried to tinder.

And the young woman burst into thunderous laughter. "Look at you!" she bellowed. "What yo wife gon' say when she see my lipstick kiss on yo head? Ha ha ha!" He reached to touch the red, and she cried, "You gon' have some explainin' to do!"

That old man closed his eyes in soundless laughter with the woman—two made one for a fleeting moment.

So did the elderly woman, who still hadn't found her Tums, laugh.

So did I, surprising myself. So did a host of travelers who had been watching the episode with me. We all laughed, gratefully. *We,* in the brief event and the silly joke of wives and kisses, were unified.

It wasn't the joke, of course. It was goodwill. It was spontaneous affection. It was the willingness of a single woman, wholly human even in the public eye—in risk and under judgment—suddenly, swiftly to love another, to honor him, to give him something graceful without hesitation or fear, something free and sweet and durable. But she gave it to us all. I won't forget her. I beg God, in such revealing moments, that I might be as generous and good as she.

There was a sanctity in the kiss of that woman.

And in this: that the man was as white as the snows of Sweden, and the woman as black as the balmy nights of Africa.

DOROTHY — IN THE CROWN OF GOD

ONE SUMMER WE TOOK Dorothy to the mountains. It was a risk, but it had become necessary to initiate certain changes in her life.

Soft Dorothy was as citified as they come, though the city she comes from is tiny. She had lived her whole life in the shelter of her parents, who kept that life very regular: sleeping, rising, eating, a little work, a load of ease, and ice cream before she went to bed each night. Almost nothing interrupted the daily round of Dorothy-affairs. She never got caught in the rain downtown. She seldom *walked* to town. She rode everywhere. She had almost never been separated from her parents.

But her father was eighty-nine years old, her mother not much younger—and Dorothy herself was forty. The clock which ticked her day so neatly was likewise ticking the lives of her parents to their ends. It was time that she should experience a real separation from them before death forced the issue and sorrow complicated everything. So we took her with us to the mountains.

But it was a risk.

Round Dorothy was ever exceedingly private. She squirreled money in secret places in her room. More valuable than money were the pictures she clipped from magazines, pictures she hid so well they shan't be found till doomsday. Her eyes would open wide with panic when little children entered her bedroom. Who can control little children? But even then Dorothy said almost nothing. She was private. She buried her thoughts; she muted her basic communication in grunts and grumbles. But she didn't have to talk, after all. Her mother knew her needs, decided her desires, spoke for her— spoke, indeed, even before Dorothy thought she had a thought. It really was time, you see, for Dorothy to step out on her own.

But round Dorothy was also exceedingly—round. The woman stood no higher than my elbow, yet was wider than I am by half at the beam. Cute little ankles, prodigious thighs, and a body as round as a medicine ball. To the *mountains* with Dorothy? Why, she could scarcely climb the stair steps one flight up.

Her eyes are slant behind their glasses; her tongue lolls on the lower lip; her chins redouble backward; her expression is generally benign and vague.

Dorothy has Down's syndrome. She is what people call "retarded." She is also Thanne's sister, my sister-in-law; and since I was to teach for several weeks at Holden Village in the Cascade Mountains of the Northwest, we took Hob in our hands and said: "Let Dorothy come with us."

Her mother swallowed painfully, considered the need, wept with a mother's solicitude, and relented. She packed for her daughter a suitcase the size of Montana (in which *she* squirreled handwritten instructions not shorter than the Book of Leviticus. For example: "Dorothy's bazooka is in her underwear. She likes to play it." Her *bazooka?* What was that? Ah, when we looked in her underwear we found her *kazoo*).

O Holden Village, hold your breath!—here comes Dorothy, the daughter of her mother. Holden, be patient and kind. We can all sacrifice a little to train this woman-child in independence, right?

Oh, and Holden? Please give us rooms low down, on a flat level with the rest of your buildings, because Dorothy is so very . . . round.

So we went to the wilds, the Wangerins six and sister Dorothy of the wide, wide eyes. It was an airplane flight from Chicago to Seattle, a car trip to the town of Chelan, a boat trip for three hours up the lake while mountains rose around us to dangerous sizes, and finally a bus trip up those mountains—miles high in the mighty, remote, foredooming mountains of God.

In Holden Village, then, Dorothy rolled her beanbag body off the bus, looked up at the craggy peaks yet higher than she, patted her bosom, and sighed: "Whew!"

The registrar met us. He pointed to our quarters. He pointed upward at an angle of forty degrees, to the top of a long road. *Whew!* We—all seven of us—bowed our heads and climbed.

"Whew!" said Dorothy. She moved as slowly as the moon. *Whew!* This medicine ball expressed herself in a variety of sighs, one for each new height as she struggled upward. And when we achieved the top of the hill—when still we stood at the bottom of the staircase that extended up to the front porch of our house—Dorothy stopped and produced a truly admirable cavalcade of sighs: "Whew! Whew! Whew!"—fanning her face, popping her eyes, and grinning. Grinning! She was Rocky Balboa at the end of his run.

Now I declare to you a wonder: Dorothy was not mute at all! She was profoundly expressive to those who had the ears to hear her.

Later, when she spied the busy ground squirrels, she paused and offered them a series of happy squeal-sighs, as if meeting with glee some long-lost relatives. When deer raised their noble necks and gazed at this round dollop of a woman, she honored them with murmurous sacred sighs as soft as lullabies. When she stepped on a slat bridge over roaring waters—which water we could see between the boards below our feet—she made a bleating sigh, and I realized how brave she was to stand so near the tumbling chaos. And when she lifted her eyes to the ring of mountains around us, and when she grew gravely still, allowing one long sigh, one eternal expulsion of breath to escape her languorous throat, I said in my soul: *Listen, my sister is praying!*

Retarded? Who is the fool that says so? This woman had an apprehension of the universe more intimate and more devout than my own. Her knowing was not troubled by extraneous thought. Dorothy had a language of genuine sophistication and of immediate response. Sighs were her words. Add to that some simple English grunts which even I could understand, and Dorothy was bilingual.

I had been to Holden Village three times before that summer, but I had never seen so well the crown surrounding it, had never seen with primal eyes until I stood with Dorothy looking up and sighing. I took squirrels to my heart, honored deer, and praised the God of supernal peaks—because of Dorothy. She was the quick one. My responses were baffled and slow. She was the one who trained me, both in seeing and in speaking. I, in the high, green tiara of the Deity—I, in simple creation—was the retarded one. How often we get it backward. How much we miss when we do!

On the second night we were there, Dorothy went up on her toes and embraced me in a mighty hug and kissed my chin and murmured, "Whew!"

I, too, said, "Whew!"

Her word meant, "What a good day!"

Mine meant, *Thank you, sweet sister, for taking me to the mountains this summer.*

"DO YOU REMEMBER THAT NIGHT?"

AT ABOUT NINE O'CLOCK in the evening—a weeknight, as I recall it—my mother telephoned from her home across several states to Evansville. She asked to talk with me.

"Hello?" I said.

She was abrupt. There were the metallic tones of urgency in her voice.

"We leave tomorrow," she said to me. "You knew that? Did you know that, Wally?"

I knew that they were preparing to travel through sub-Saharan Africa, my parents together, but no: I hadn't known that their departure was so close upon them.

"Tomorrow," I said.

"Tomorrow," she repeated. "Flight leaves at eight thirty-six in the morning."

Mom was breathing heavily, as if they meant to run the distance and were getting a head start now. Or else as if she were terrified of the prospect. What time was it for her right now? Shouldn't she be in bed?

But Mom and Dad had already spent a great portion of their lives in Hong Kong, where Dad established a Christian college and Mom taught Chinese children. At various points in my father's career they had traveled overseas, and by many means had they gone. Why would my mother be fearful now?

"Wally? Are you listening to me? Are you paying attention?"

"Yes, Mom. Of course I am."

During this particular journey my father would act as an educational consultant for a host of Christian schools, spending time at each one, assessing, discussing, leading workshops. Preaching. My father preached almost everywhere he went. He considered these assignments late in his career to be "Missionary Journeys." He drew quiet parallels between his labors and St. Paul's.

"Wally?"

"What."

"Do you remember that night—?"

She paused. For an instant she could not continue. But my mother is ever verbal, as quick as scissors with her words, and fiery, too.

"Mom. What are you—"

"Do you remember what you said to me?" she demanded.

"But what night do you—"

"The night in the dining room—" she overspoke my words, denying me any speculation about which night she had in mind. "We were in the dining room. After supper. You, home from school," she rushed to the point. "You caught your jacket on the screendoor. Wally! Do you remember what you said to me?"

Ahhhhh. *That* night.

Our memories are remarkable and immediate, my mother's and mine. And a single detail can pitch us at once and together into the furnace of any past event. We hit the coals walking, as did Shadrach, Meshach, and Abednego.

Do you remember what you said to me?

Yes. Yes.

Mostly, when my mother screamed at me, I was mute, incapable of *any* response, let alone a loud one or a reasoned one. Her force blew language straight out of my head. I couldn't even think a word, let alone utter it, so consumed was I by the guilt of her accusations, so confused by the dizzying, impossible leaps of her logic. She was a square-set woman in those days, a solid physical presence. And her words, under pressure of her emotions, shot like jets of flame into my soul. She was a poet of the thrilling, ripping image, and I was torn, and I burned before her.

But on that particular night I had found my voice. Hoarsely I had shouted back at her. And the thing I said was a thing I had been contemplating for a long time. I suppose it had been packaged and prepared for delivery, though I knew nothing of such internal preparations.

The thing I yelled at her had been born of a fathomless sorrow in me. For it seemed to me that my mother did not truly believe in the grace of God. For she never confessed a sin of her own—not, at least, in my presence nor in our long relationship. And anything that even betokened a personal fault on her part would send her into furies of retaliation and counter accusations. *But,* I thought to myself, *if only she would confess.* She would then be forgiven, and her torments, her internal contradictions could finally be eased. The fire extinguished, the furnace would cool. In fact, she *was* forgiven, could she know it. But first . . .

Ah, mother, the yearning rose from an ineffable love, *God can make you peaceful.*

On that night of screaming, I raised my own voice and the thing got said.

I remember an autumn weekend. Friday evening. Saturday. Most of the rest of the family is absent, out of the house or out of the room. Whatever the case, they do not appear in my memory. There are but the two of us, dirty dishes on the table, Mom still sitting at her place, I standing across the table. I am wearing a light windbreaker. The light seems impossibly bright.

As she scolds me, she becomes more and more agitated. I think we're discussing the amount of time I do and do not spend at home.

I utter excuses. I speak in my own defense.

But every effort on my account bedevils my mother the more. She slaps the table with the flat of her hand. Finally she rises up, screaming, screaming.

And I can't bear the look in her face. Or the cut of her words. And to tell it truly, it is not only the personal assault that drowns me and leaves me breathless, it is also the howling desolations of my mother's soul.

"Mom!" I cry it as loudly as I can: "I have already forgiven you!" I turn. I start to escape the dining room. I can't now recall whether she is screaming still, or else has fallen silent, but I *think* she's screaming, for everything in me yearns to run away. I reach the back door. I open it. I'm clumsy. I can't jerk the screen door open.

"I have already forgiven you!" I shout, scarcely aware of the source of these words. And I shout: "You just don't know it yet!"

The pocket of my windbreaker catches on the screendoor handle. I am so desperate to run, it tears, and I go.

"Do you remember what you said to me?" my mother asked, so many years after that night, mere hours before she and my father took off for Africa, and who knew when they would be home again.

Her telephone voice was urgent, headlong.

Do you remember?

And I—my head lowered, my left hand cupping the mouthpiece of the telephone, my voice subdued, and my heart made vulnerable all over again—I answered in the darkness, "Yes. I remember."

There was a beat of silence. I was in my study. The study door was closed. That's why the room was dark. Thanne was in the kitchen.

"Well," said my mother with this persistent urgency, "did you mean it? Did you mean what you said to me?"

And although I was no longer that boy, trembling in a dining room so brightly lit with lights and fires and feelings; though I could only recall, not actually feel, the mood with which the boy first spoke the words, I said, "Yes."

"Well, then," my mother said. "So, then. Good. Fine. All right."

She hung up. I heard the distant click.

RISE, DOROTHY, RISE

GENUINE LOVE IS DEFINED by this, that it is prepared to sacrifice itself for the sake of the beloved.

Sham love, on the other hand, makes *itself* the motive, the cause and the end of relationship. Sham love may know "sacrifice," but only as a means to reach some goal of its own. It says, "Since I have given up so much for you, now you owe me..." There is no giving without some getting, even if that which is gotten is merely public praise or the sweet internal feeling: *What a good person am I!*

Genuine love serves. Neither requiring nor expecting something in return. Its character is, simply, to serve—and those who stumble against these twin axioms of sacrifice and service will likewise stumble against the cross. They will fall down crying, "Scandal!"

Sham love stumbles.

Sham love may *think* it desires to serve the beloved; in fact, it desires only (and precisely) the beloved for itself. It desires his company, her person—some respondent love. So its service is not an end in itself. Sham love may perform the most difficult services, things its beloved shall absolutely need—until she becomes dependent upon them and thereby bound unto her "servant," her benefactor. Do you see? Sham love fulfills itself in the end by possessing the other.

Genuine love has one goal only: the health and honor, the full flowering and the *freedom* of the beloved. It serves her that she might become her own most beautiful self. It seeks the rose within the bud, and then—when all the world sees but a nubble—it nourishes that bud with rain and the richness of its own self. This is holy sacrifice, the outpouring of one self upon another, until that other opens up and blossoms. Genuine love rejoices when the beloved is finally lovely and perfectly free.

Sham love never perceives the image intrinsic within the other. Rather, it makes up its own image of what she ought to be according to its own designs, then imposes this fiction upon her. When she does not conform (well, she can't: she is *herself,* not *his* self) sham love might remain resolutely blind to what she is and pretend that *she* has conformed, imprisoning her within its restrictive lie. Or else it will blame her for the failure: "I'm so disappointed in you!" Thus justified, sham love will try harder to force conformity, or will reject her altogether. In either case, it confesses no wrong. It believes it has *been* wronged.

One of the plainest signs of sham love is self-pity.

Another is fear of freedom.

Since the goal of sham love is itself, it must control the beloved. In fact, it measures her love by the amount of obedience she gives its will. Therefore, though genuine love takes a genuine joy in the free flight of the beloved, sham love is angered by her slightest act of independence; angered first, then threatened; then frightened by the independence that bodes separation; and finally, if she has flown indeed, sham love falls into the despair of the unfulfilled.

Listen to the songs of the world and the language it uses for love. How often the point of the song is the singer! Listen to the wisdom of the world: "Feeling good about myself, yeah! Satisfaction is my birthright, and my worth you must acknowledge, just because I AM." Such a demand—though it makes a worldly sense—is exactly the opposite of sacred love, for it makes a god of the self.

It must always be offended by the cross.

But listen, and I will show you a more excellent way.

More than forty years ago my parents-in-law brought Dorothy into the world—their thirteenth child, an infant afflicted with Down's syndrome. Because of her mental incapacity, they chose to keep her at home; and though she learned much and went forth to work each day, they lavished upon her more service than any other child required. In fact, her presence and her need required her parents to continue *as* parents long after they might have been taking their ease. Martin added ninety years to his age and still was parenting a child; Gertrude added eighty-four. But this is love, that they served with unceasing, uncomplaining devotion for forty-one years.

But this, too, is genuine love: that finally they had to stop serving her.

Dorothy has moved into a group home established for the mentally handicapped. She received her own room, her own place in life. She picked out her own wallpaper and curtains—and all this was pure delight to her. She was free.

But her mother was weeping. And her father, full of love, was solemn. Suddenly they weren't parents any more. They were not needed as they had been. They had sacrificed, for their daughter's sake, their significant reason to *be*, had sacrificed something of their own identities. This is love. The emptiness of the house; the release of its sometime sweet inhabitant, who had been life and focus for old eyes; the farewell of the heart: "Good-bye, good-bye, Dorothy"— this is love.

But Gertrude and Martin knew how close they were to dying. They knew that Dorothy would suffer a double trauma should they die while she was still beside them, since any new home would then be ruined by the reason for going and the grieving that brought her there. So Gertrude and Martin chose to bear the grief of departure themselves, while Dorothy could feel a full, untroubled joy in it. This is a gift she may never comprehend. This is her parents' personal sacrifice. This is love.

Just before she was driven away, they kissed her. Martin moved slowly in a walker. Gertrude, for a weak heart, puffed small puffs of air. Dorothy clambered into the car without a second thought, grinned, and waved brightly. Gertrude rushed back into the house, embarrassed by her tears. Martin bent into the car window. "Be good," the old man whispered. "Be good, Dorothy. Good-bye."

And then he, too, wept.

But he let her go. The bud was becoming a rose. The rains that washed and watered her may never see this blossom blow. They serve, and then they sink into the earth. This is a genuine love.

THE GRANDPARENT, FINALLY, OF MANY

A NOAH TREE

BRAVELY, DRAMATICALLY I DECLARED to the woman at Samuelson's Nursery, "I want to purchase a Noah Tree. Does Samuelson's have a Noah Tree?"

She frowned, not even pretending that such a thing existed.

"He should be a beautiful tree," I fairly sang the description: "straight-stemmed, full of promise for the strength and the height of his maturity. For he will carry me, one day!"

At my approach the woman had removed her gloves to serve me. Now, wordlessly, she began to put them on again.

So I came down from my foolishness. "Forgive me," I said. "I have a grandson, two months old. Our first, you know. And I want to plant a tree in his name." I grinned hard, helplessly. "In the name of Noah Martin!"

And I knew the color of my tree instinctively.

"Do you have," I said, "a flaming maple?"

I bought the tree on Wednesday.

All day Thursday I dug a great pit on the highest ground in the field behind our house. I lined my pit with a rich mulch and a good black earth. I watered both the root-ball of the maple and the soil that would receive it. And then, myself a rain of sweating, I rolled the ball into the pit and filled it layer-by-layer with more black earth.

I delighted in the labor.

On Friday our daughter Mary came to town with her husband John and their child, our grandchild, Noah Martin Sauger. They took a bedroom. I said, "Come outside."

I showed them the tree. Baby Noah was oblivious, but his parents appreciated the work. The Noah Tree stood twelve feet high, its stem two inches in diameter, its red leaves spread like a double umbrella just above our heads.

Friends from Evansville showed up on Saturday—many of these past members of the Sounds of Grace, our remarkable choir. All of the rest of the family—Thanne's and mine—came too: Joseph from Minneapolis with his fiancée, Catherine Preus; Matthew, up from Atlanta; Talitha and her fiancée, Ray Washington from Connecticut. These two were in graduate school together. They had come home to marry.

In fact, their wedding was much the public center of our gathering, this particular weekend in May, 1998. On Saturday afternoon Talitha and Ray were married here in Valparaiso at Christ Lutheran Church. I preached. Oh, how close to the gates I stood that weekend: for under my formal ministrations, and in the rituals of our worship, generations and generations were meeting and weaving together. I was entering the golden age of my vocation with a nearly speechless joy: I preached.

And then, on Sunday morning, I drew fresh well-water into a basin. I bore the basin to a low table in our living room. I set a cross before, and lit two candles on either side of, the water.

And, thus prepared, I called together the whole company of family and friends, to witness the baptism of our grandson, Noah Martin.

Although I've never found it written down, by way of the oral traditions of African-Americans I know a certain ritual observed by grandmother slaves in the deep and humid, long-ago South. Twice the living grandchildren described the ritual to me. And though the details differed between my two story tellers, the human sadness and the grave admiration of their telling was the same.

It was a ritual involving of infants and trees. It was performed on hidden ground in perfect secrecy; the custom was the spiritual use of material things; it was a brave assault on time and space and

207 Noah Tree 207

separations; and it fought the sorrow of a certain loss with a stern, perpetual union—and with a Something Dear To Do.

Here, briefly, is what I heard:

That shortly before a slave woman was to give birth, she was led by the grandmother slaves into the woods, to a clearing in the woods where there grew a tended and nurtured grove of trees, to a tub of water in that clearing. At night under moonlight, the old women washed the younger one in that tub. They saved the water.

That, in the same night, a seedling was planted at the edge of the grove, where trees of every age and species could be found, saplings and the mossy oaks tended well together.

That hard labor brought this woman and all the grandmothers back to the grove and to the tub and to that water, waiting.

That she bore her baby in the tub, and all the fluids of this parturition mingled with the waters of her own washing; yes, and the afterbirth, too.

That the placenta was buried near the root of the seedling planted, and the soup of birthing was poured over all.

And that the infant and the tree bore the very same name together. Not two same names for two beings, one rooted and one walking. No: it was one name, one spirit in two manifestations.

And why would the grandmothers go to such a trouble? And why did they return regularly to this grove, to prune and to mulch, to protect it and to stand in its shade?

Because this was the grove of the generations of their children. Every tree received the same nursing as did the child whose spirit dwelt within that tree; and the love of the grandmothers was fed to the fleshy mouth as to the woody one, both as one. They kissed the baby when he grew a child. They taught the fresh young woman of blood and bearing. They loved the flesh while flesh was with them still. But ever and ever they lived against the day when that sweet flesh would be taken from them and the two would be torn asunder. For the slaves were sold, and these grandmothers had no control over the sale, and the children lost would surely *suffer* the lostness, too—aliens in the universe.

Aliens, except for this: that their spirits still had a dwelling place near the love and the nourishment of home.

For the grandmothers had a Something Dear To Do, by which to keep a fierce, abiding union. Daily they cared for the trees, caring thereby for the souls of their grandbabies. Here were their children's symbols close to hand.

And the young men lost, and the young women sold into Midianite hands—they knew. They had in memory the tree, the place where their grandmothers were rendering service. And they need never doubt the service! Someone still was stroking their souls and begging the Heavenly Father on their behalf. Wherever else they went, their home remained their home. And the hard link was the tree.

Maintaining that grove maintained the family in spite of the knives of time and space, and the strikes of the unkind powers of this world.

Moreover, I learned from a Jewish friend that he and many Jews balance the circumcision of their sons by planting trees for their daughters. It becomes her own placement among the People, as trees in nature are placed. Her life, its life: green beneath the summer's sun, growing, a citizen of every weather—with mountains and hills, with fruit trees and all cedars praising the name of the Lord!

So the Sunday morning living room was crowded soon with our People. I stood at the little table that bore the basin of water, and prayed a prayer.

Catherine Preus sat down at the piano. She made chords sound like falling water, and then we, all of us, sang a hymn together. And because the voices from Grace Church were among us, we were angels hovering at the baby's shoulders.

We sang: *Thy holy wings, O Savior, Spread gently over me.*

Our words were lifted on behalf of baby Noah, who could not utter a word for himself: *And let me rest securely, Through good and ill with thee.*

Noah slept. Asleep, his eyes never opening, Noah stretched and yawned, and the sunlight flooded his mouth, and still we sang: *O be my strength and portion, My rock and hiding place . . .*

Tears sprang up in my daughter's eyes, Mary the mother still holding her baby in arms. I motioned her to stand and come forward. She did. John did. The baby did, while we sang: *And let my every moment Be lived within thy grace.*

Then Mary could not stop crying. Nor could John. And Grandma Thanne's eyelashes sparkled with her gladness. And before all the people, I made floods of water fall upon my grandson's head, saying, "Noah Martin, I baptize you in the name of the Father, and of the Son, and of the Holy Spirit."

Loud clapping exploded in our living room, and it seemed to me that every pair of hands was a pair of wings beating the air as when great flocks of birds take flight.

I lifted the bowl of baptismal water in my own hands. I wound my way through the crowd, then through the kitchen and out our back door, and Mary came beside me, and Thanne was carrying Noah now, and the angels followed as we processed to the field behind our house, and to the flaming maple waiting there.

The people sang spontaneously in the sunlight:

"O let me nestle near thee
Within thy downy breast
Where I will find sweet comfort
And peace within thy nest."

As we approached the tree, I whispered to Thanne to stand beneath its shadow. The tree would protect the baby from the harsher sunlight.

The rest came through the field. They gathered in a circle, singing:

"Oh, close thy wings around me
And keep me safely there;
For I am but a newborn
And need thy tender care."

Thanne elevated the child as high as she could. Noah went up fearlessly. The maple leaves crowned him with fire beneath a cobalt sky. Wind tousled us all. Then Grandpa, the preacher, spoke of the Tree of Life at the beginning of time, that tree which was shut against us when we had sinned by eating the fruit of another tree. Grandpa poured a little of the baptismal water at the roots of the maple.

Next the preacher spoke of the tree at the center of time, upon which Christ hung as the curse of God, upon which Jesus poured his red, red blood, to win us life again. And at the roots of the maple I poured a little more water.

Finally I spoke of the Tree of Life, now awaiting us all at the end of time.

"Awaiting you, my blessed grandson," I said.

I stooped and poured the rest of the water of Noah's second birth at the wooden mouth of Noah's tree.

When I am done writing today, I will get up from my desk and lock my studio door and walk home over the field in which my grandson's tree still stands, still grows, is more than twice my height. There are four such trees in the field, now: a willow, a fir, a blue spruce, and the maple. I pause as I pass them. For not one of our grandchildren lives nearby; and who knows where their parents will take them in the future, or what their destinies shall do to them. And I am growing older. I travel less. I count my remaining years. I keep close to home.

But in these trees are the spirits of my grandchildren invested, and by each tree I am reminded that the time and the space that takes them away cannot finally sunder the cords of my compassion for them. No. And should they go so far from me that I cannot hear their voices at all, yet this relationship shall supercede the unkindness of the slavers of this world, surely. Surely!

For even as I have named the trees, God has named my grand-children one by one! And the name God gave them, every one, is "My Delight Is In You," and "You Are My Child."

Yea, though Noah should take the wings of the morning and dwell in the uttermost parts of the sea, even there the shadow of the Savior's tree shall find him and cover him.

A PSALM: GOD IN A GRANDCHILD, SMILING

Omnipotens sempiterne Deus!
Almighty God, the Everlasting, Thou!
I cannot look steadfastly at the sun and not go blind. Holiness exceeds my sight—though I know it is, and I know thou art.

Aeterne Deus omnium rerum Creator!
Thou art above all created things.
To everything made, thou art the Other. Greater than thee there is no world; in thee all worlds have being; and I take my trivial, mortal way upon the smallest sphere of all. How shall I hope to see thee and not to die?

Lux Mundi!
But in thy mercy:
Thou shinest down upon the things that thou hast made. They brighten in thy light. Every morning they reflect thee. I wake to an effulgence of mirrors, and lo: I see.

Misericors Deus!
For my sake, for my poor fleshly sight:
Thou changest thy terrible holiness here before me into glory—the visible light, the doxology I can see. I rise and look around, and I cry praise to thee.

Deus, incommutabilis virtus, lumen aeternum!
From thee to me it is a mighty diminution:
Ever the same, thou makest thy presence manifest in things that

are both mutable and common. But from me to thee it is epiphany: gazing at things most common, suddenly I see thy light, thy glory, and thy face.

Nobiscum Deus!
Then:
What shall I say to thee but *Deo Gratias?* Thanks be to God!

Deo Gratias!
For the dew that damps the morning grasses is a baptism, always, always renewing the earth. And the air remembers that once it ushered down the dove that was the breath of God. And I myself inhale the rinsed spirit of the morning air and I, too, am renewed.

Deo Gratias!
For dawn, in the chalices of the clouds, brims them with a bloody wine, a running crimson. And this is a sign to me. The sun is coming.

Deo Gratias!
For the sun, when it breaks at the horizon, transfigures every thing. And this is a gift to me. For the transfiguration itself persuades my soul of sunrise.

Jesui filii Dei, gratias!
For I have seen a baby sleeping in a shaft of sunlight, and behold: in the curve of every eyelash was a small sun cupped. And from these fringes tiny rays shot forth to sting me. Wherefore sunrise at the far horizon was sunrise near me in this infant.

Et verbum caro factum est—
For the baby suddenly opened her mouth and yawned. And into that pink cavern rushed the sunlight, trembling and flashing like a living thing. But it was thee, bright God, in the mouth of a mortal infant.

"Ecce ego vobiscum sum—"

For the baby woke to the morning and saw me close beside her, and she smiled.

Ah, God! What an epiphany of smiling that was! My own transfiguration! For this was the primal light, the glory of the morning, thy splendor and thy face before me come.

Deo gratias, cuius gloria!

Then glory be to thee, Father, Son, and Holy Spirit, as it was in the beginning, is now, and ever shall be, *saecula saeculorum.*

Amen.

MY NAME IS DOROTHY BOHLMANN

Dear Dorothy:

Just last Saturday we gathered at Mom and Dad Bohlmann's to celebrate Independence Day. You came—you and all your mates from group home, both the staff and the "handicapped" inhabitants. Thanne and I were there too, of course, with four other Bohlmann "children" and their spouses. They all have spouses. All your mother's children married—except two. Of the fourteen children she bore, only two did not leave home to marry and to bear children of their own. But Raymond died when he was an infant, more than half a century ago.

And you have Down's syndrome.

Dorothy, did you ever stop enjoying the weddings of your many siblings? Did you ever think it was your turn to be given such attention, such a beautiful day, and such a good good-bye? And then did it ever seem that the ceremony everyone else received had been denied to you alone? The last child to leave left nearly twenty years ago. But you stayed. Did you watch and wait in yearning? Did yearning ever turn to envy, and envy into sorrow?

It is my instinct that you did. I think you, too, in the natural course of growing older, wanted to marry. It's only an instinct. You never spoke. For years and years you made your feelings known in tears or smiles or fussy grunts—or sighs. You said "Whew" a thousand ways. But no words.

Well, and it is also my instinct that having been granted no choice in something so universally human, you exercised choice in one of the few areas over which no one had control but you. You could not choose not to eat, of course. And your mother insisted on choosing *what* you ate, *what* you wore, *where* you went, *how*

215

you got there, *when* you would come home. I think you marked off a tiny area of independence by withdrawing into silence. No one could reach you there.

Dorothy, I think there was a part of you that *chose* not to talk.

So, on the Fourth of July last week, we "normal" folks stood on the library lawn in Watseka, Illinois, and watched a parade in which the whole town participated. Your housemates dressed like clowns and strode the street with great solemnity, staring straight ahead—oh, so obedient and so earnest!

Then we gathered in Mom's backyard under a splendid blue Midwestern sky. We gave thanks to God for independence and for freedom. We sang "God Bless America." We prayed. We ate. You sat in state, it seemed to me, receiving the attentions of many friends, the only one related to everyone there—and then it dawned on me how you are the hinge that joins two families, for you are a Bohlmann, and you are the only Bohlmann in the group home. If the Wangerins and the Bohlmanns had gathered, then Thanne would have been the hinge between two families because she married me. Because she left her home and I left mine and we made a new home together, joining two.

I gazed long at you that afternoon, dear sister, and I said in my soul, *No, but Dorothy did leave her mother and her father to cleave unto others, and they have made a new home together—*

Oh, Dorothy, how you have changed!

Look at you, Lady: here comes Donny of the group home, whizzing through the yard (Donny, whose face is as aerodynamic as a 747, is always whizzing); he suddenly stops to hug you and ask how you are doing, seriously searches your eyes for a whole second, then is seized with another spasm of speed, and whizzes on. Donny wears an old World-War-One-flying-ace hat with earflaps. And you? You accept his adoration as something natural to him and due to you. Then you happen to catch me watching you. So you wave a little wind into your face and you smile back at me and you sigh, "Whew, whew!"—as if to say, *That's Donny. He'll take your breath away.*

Do you remember when we went to the mountains together? That was four years ago. You still make the silly sigh you made then, but you scarcely *need* to any more. You've lost roundness! Motion is easier now than before. The new home which you have made with others has made you a healthier woman. Independence. I said in my soul, *No, Dorothy's no different from any child of Gertrude after all.* Independence is the beginning of health, an absolutely necessary thing.

Yet Gertrude suffered when you left her. That was two years ago. And since you were the last to leave of her fourteen, it was, I believe, as if all fourteen symbolically left with you; motherhood itself departed Gertrude when you did. How long did it take her to reconcile herself? She kept appearing in your new home, still making decisions for you, rearranging your clothes in the dresser drawers, still instructing you in what to wear. Well, and then you made silence your privacy: you thrust out your lip and folded your arms, and sometimes you wore exactly what you wanted to wear, though it wounded and outraged your poor mother. For something so wrong as this, someone must be at fault. Well, so she'd blame the staff of the group home for letting you get away with murder. Well, so everyone was upset for a while. Independence is a terrible thing. It tears from those who are left behind their very reason for being. It causes a nearly catastrophic loneliness. It was very hard on Mom. Recently I wrote that she has stopped crying about your absence. She wrote back straightway to tell me I was wrong. She still cries.

She's eighty-seven this year. What a change she had to sustain in her old age! Her heart is weak, this mother of many, this grandmother of multitudes. It cannot be long before she and Martin shall die. They know that. They speak of it, not always peacefully but always, always faithfully. She trembles when she moves too much. Martin is ninety-two. He drags a walker slowly. He had to lean on his son's arm in order to come down the porch stairs into the yard for our Independence Day picnic, and there he sat in a wheelchair making jokes. Both of your parents have minds as lucid as your own heart is lucid, Dorothy. Yes, Gertrude still cries for you. Perhaps she always will. And I think you know that, don't you?

I watched you throughout the length of a long, lazy afternoon. And before the Midwestern sun had set, sweet sister, I saw you do two marvelous things.

One was new and astonishing. It took my breath away. It made me know how much you've grown and how good "marriage" has been for you. The other was natural unto you, no change at all, the same sort of thing you've been doing all your life but no less marvelous for that.

In the midst of the day's activity, I heard something. I heard you. Under the noises of your housemates, who speak a yowling sort of English, who laugh with perfect delight and lolling tongues, who rush hither and yon as if accomplishing some business so urgent the sky would fall without it; under the hubbub of eating and gossip and fire-cracking, the dashing of the children; under the long, slow snoozing of the sun, I heard a murmuring. I looked and saw that your spirit had withdrawn into its private vale, and I thought that the day had become too much for you again. But then I saw your lips move. You were repeating the same soft sentence over and over.

Dorothy, you were speaking! Sister, you were talking—although you seemed oblivious of the loud celebration all around you: talking to yourself, then.

Well, I crept near you to hear you the better but slowly, slowly, so that my coming would not disturb the moment nor destroy the quiet sentence. And then it was you who took my breath away.

With your head bent as if contemplating some complicated thing, gazing into your two palms upturned in your lap, scarcely moving your lips, you were murmuring, "My name is Dorothy

Bohlmann. My name is Dorothy Bohlmann. My name is Dorothy Bohlmann—"

I said in my soul, *This woman is free! This woman is whole! No, she is in nothing diminished. She is the equal of any child of Gertrude and Martin, the peer of any child of God.*

Thirteen children indeed did leave to make new homes for themselves and new lives, too. Only Raymond did not. You did. The only difference between you and your siblings is that you were the last to go and bore the greater burden therefore. But now you, Dorothy, are fully adult. Let no one lisp when they speak to you. Let no one simplify speech and exaggerate their tone as if they were talking to a child of small understanding. In that sense you are no child at all.

And in another sense you are more mature than most of my acquaintances.

Near the end of the day, after the rest of the group home had departed, leaving you with us for the night, after the yard had been cleaned and while we sat chatting, entering evening, suddenly Mom cried out in pain and grabbed her leg. All her children rushed toward her. "No!" she said, waving people back and trying to laugh the pain away, but it kept returning in stabs and she couldn't help crying out again: "Oh! *Oh, NO!*"

It had been a hard day. Mom doesn't know how to quit. Moreover the party had been her idea. She wanted to make some gesture of thanksgiving to the staff of the group home. She wanted somehow to say that she didn't blame them any more. Gertrude is making peace. Your mother, Dorothy, is laboring to let you go. I think she is granting you your liberty. It was a day made hard, then, as much by the work of the heart as of the body.

"Ow!" she cried. Tears broke down her cheeks.

Immediately your face twisted with anxiety. You felt your mother's pain. It is your skill immediately to enter another soul and to feel precisely what that one feels.

And you love your mother.

Gertrude allowed Thanne to come near her. It was a severe muscle spasm in her leg; it wanted a hard massage. And you. You crept near your mother, too, patting and patting her leg with your small hand, you and Thanne, sisters side by side: where Thanne's hands went your hand followed, your eyes deep within your mother's eyes—and that, Dorothy, is as marvelous as anything you've ever done, because of the unsullied love it revealed, but then it is exactly what you have done all your life. It is natural to you. Independence has not changed sympathy. Independence does not cancel love. It transfigures it, making it purely a gift.

So your touch eased your mother like a medicine.

And I said in my soul, *No, but Dorothy is different from us after all. She is better. She loves more quickly and with less confusion.*

Ah, Dorothy, I think God honors hearts more than brains. You are the image of God in my world. In you the best of the child continues, while the best of adulthood emerges. Your declaration of independence never stole a state nor severed a nation nor warred against another soul. It only allowed you to return love for love in greater measure than before.

I love you, my sister.

Walt

DUST

I yearn
To curl in the corner
Of death's eye:
Death's deep eye.
When he blinks
I am enclosed,
And I am washed
With weeping.

ONE MAN ON A
TRACTOR, FAR AWAY

April 28, 1995:

I've opened a small suitcase on the bed. The window shades are pulled. They usually are, night and day. Their white translucence, though, allows a fine spring light in the bedroom; and as I move from the closet to the dresser, gathering clothes for packing, I feel glad anticipations about the weekend.

It's Friday. Early afternoon. In forty-five minutes I will leave town for Wheaton College in Illinois where one of my stories is to receive its first public performance. As good as that—better than that, actually—I'm to meet one of my best friends there, whose full-length play will also be performed. His piece is the real feature of Wheaton's theater festival; mine's a private excitement.

My friend's name is David McFadzean. The director at Wheaton is Jim Young, soft-spoken, with talent as deep as tree roots.

I'm going to drive. I'll be back on Sunday.

So, then: two clean shirts, fresh underwear, a pair of dark slacks; my shaving kit is in the bathroom. . . .

Just as I burst from the bathroom, Thanne appears at the top of the stairs. She lets me rush past her, then follows into the bedroom. She's moving slowly. Thanne will often suspend her work while I get ready for some extended trip. She'll say good-bye in the driveway.

"You think I'll need my raincoat?"

She doesn't answer.

"Thanne?"

I glance at her. No, her slowness now is not a preparation for "Good-bye." She hasn't sat. My wife is gazing at the window

222

shades as if they were open and the world lay visible before her. Her head is drawn back. There are small bunches of flesh at the corners of her lips.

"Thanne?"

For a moment she stands unmoving. The shades *are* pulled; there *is* no world before her. There's nothing to see. Her face is illuminated by a diffusion of light. I stuff the shaving kit into my suitcase. I will say her name again, with greater emphasis—but then she speaks in a dreaming murmur: "Wally."

"Yes? What?"

Now Thanne turns and turns on me the same wondering gaze she gave the window shade.

"Dad's gone," she says.

"Ah."

There is no explanation for this, but I understand the sense of her words immediately, completely. I don't ask her to elaborate. There is no compulsion in me toward surprise or shock. Rather, I scrutinize the woman carefully, to see how she is herself responding to this . . . this, what? Act of God?

Dad's gone.

But she stands as erect as first I ever saw her, and the cast of her neck and head make her seem a Grecian column to hold the roofs of temples. Except for the line between her eyebrows, her countenance is composed.

"Thanne?"

I'm asking after her state of being. I would add, *How are you?*—except she thinks I'm asking for details, and answers first.

Softly, as if all this were a wonder to her, Thanne draws me the picture in her mind. "Mom says it was just after lunch. They'd come back to their rooms. Dad had shifted himself from the wheelchair into his TV chair. Mom wasn't paying any attention. She was just about to sit, when Dad took three quick breaths . . . and then he was gone."

I step toward her now. I gather the woman into my arms. I take her face against my throat, and we stand still. She is not crying. She is deeply quiet.

My wife's father, Martin Bohlmann, has just died. This is the first of our four parents to go.

Softly, still with that note of awe-ful wonder, Thanne adds one more detail.

"Mom's says it's a good thing Dad took those three breaths, and that they were loud. Otherwise she'd have talked to a dead man till suppertime."

Spring, 1967:

The farmer was not a talky man. Not ever, I suppose—though when I first met him I assumed that the size and the noise of his family didn't permit him time to talk.

At the age of twenty-three I drove west from Ohio to the flat, black farmland of eastern Illinois, there to visit the Bohlmann farm, to seek approval of the Bohlmann parents, and to court the Bohlmann daughter named Ruthanne.

On a Friday evening we sat down to supper in the spacious kitchen. The day had been balmy. I remember that the kitchen door stood open to the porch, so that breezes stole in behind me. The air was warm and rich and loamy. Jonquils and daffodils were in bloom, the tulip beds about to pop, the ground as yet uncultivated. I'd been a city boy all my life. I wanted to weep for the perfect sense of sufficiency which this world provided me.

There were eight of us at the table, though it could accommodate fifteen at least. Martin and Gertrude had brought forth fourteen children. They buried one in infancy and now had watched nearly all the others depart for college. Ruthanne was the tenth child born to them, the fifth from the last.

The farmer bowed his head. "Come!" he said with surprising force, then lowered his voice for the rest of the prayer: "COME, Lord Jesus, be our guest. . . ."

I soon learned that the first word was something like a gong, alerting the rest of his huge family to the sacred duty now begun.

Apart from that commanding "Come," Martin's praying and his manner both were mild. His hair, on the other hand—aimed at me from the bowed head at the other end of the table—constituted a fierce aggression. It never would comb down, but stood up and stabbed like bayonets in defiance.

As soon as the prayer was done, a hard, clattering silence overtook the table, while every Bohlmann concentrated on filling up their plates.

Potatoes and vegetables had been raised in the kitchen garden. Popcorn, too. Milk came from Bohlmann cows. There'd been a time when the hog was hung up on a chilly autumn morning and butchered in the barn door, giving cracklings to the family, hams and chops and sausages and lard. Gertrude used the lard for the wedding cakes she baked to earn spending money. The Bohlmanns owned neither the land they worked nor the house they slept in. They rented. They never paid income tax, since their annual income never approached a taxable figure. For them it was a short distance from the earth to their stomachs—and back to earth again. Thanne recalls the cold two-holer on snowy winter mornings.

Martin ate that meal mostly in silence. But so did he eat all his meals, and so did he live most of his life: in silence.

When he was done, he slipped a toothpick into the corner of his mouth, read aloud a brief devotion for our general benefit, pushed back his chair, stood up, and walked outside.

I followed him. I think I thought I'd talk with him, persuade him of the honor of my intentions. But Martin moved in the sort of solitude which, it seemed to my young self, admitted no foolish intrusions. And once outside, he kept on walking. So I lingered in the yard and watched, following no farther than that.

In twilight the farmer, clad in clean coveralls, strolled westward into the field immediately beyond the yard. He paused. He stood silhouette, the deep green sky framing his body with such precision that I could see the toothpick twiddling between his lips. His hair was as stiff and wild as a thicket, the great blade of his nose majestic.

Soon Martin knelt on one knee. He reached down and gathered a handful of dirt. He lifted it, then sifted the lumpish dust through his fingers onto the palm of his other hand. Suddenly he brought both hands to his face and inhaled. The toothpick got switched to the side; Martin touched the tip of his tongue to the earth. Then he rose again. He softly clapped his two hands clean, then slipped them behind the bib of his coveralls, and there he stood, straight up, gazing across the field, his form as black as iron in the gloaming, his elbows forming the joints of folded wings—and I thought: *How peaceful! How completely peaceful is this man.*

It caused in me a sort of sadness, a nameless elemental yearning.

April 29, 1995:

I am in Wheaton with David McFadzean, sitting at a small table in the college snack bar. I drove my little pickup here, while Thanne drove the mini-van south into the Illinois farm country of her childhood. She's with her mother and her siblings in Watseka, arranging for her father's funeral, which has been scheduled for Monday. Thanne has already contacted our own children, to see which will be able to attend the funeral. They will all be there—at least for the wake on Sunday.

Since there's little I can do for Martin now, and since Thanne herself is surrounded by a small city of Bohlmann's, we decided I should keep my appointments after all. And I have. But I move as something of an alien here. I'm morbidly conscious of my body, the thing I live in, as if it were a bunting concealing my truer self. No, that's not quite accurate: rather, my body is the heavy thing I bear wherever I go, as if it were a prison of severe limitations. And here's the irony: to lose it or to leave it is to die.

Last night the Wheaton College Theater Department performed my story, "One In A Velvet Gown." It's a melancholy piece, based on personal boyhood experience. Watching it, I became a watcher of my past, departed self.

We're going to watch David's play tonight. He tells me it's still a work in progress. He grins, suddenly conscious of what he's doing. He's preparing the both of us to forgive the flaws he fears we'll see.

"How's Thanne," he says. This is a running joke: "I'd rather be talking to her, not you!" His eyes blink flat with a false sincerity.

I swallow coffee and surprise myself by saying, "He can't be gone."

"What?" David tucks his chin into his neck and curls a lip of wry query: "Whaaat?" He thinks I'm giving him joke for joke.

I say, "Thanne's Dad died yesterday," and then I feel terrible. It's a crude, stupid way to announce such a thing. But this is how separate I feel: when David snaps to a confused sobriety, I don't apologize. I don't say anything. I don't even acknowledge his gestures of sympathy—or if I do, I don't *know* that I do.

For as soon as I uttered that sentence of death out loud, I realized I meant much more than Martin's physical departure. I meant the man's entire way of life, his perfect peace in the universe. And now my spirit is breathless at so tremendous a loss. For if *these* are gone, than the world has become a dangerous place altogether.

What? And shall all my fears return again, making me an alien wherever I go?

1900–1950:

Martin Bohlmann was born with the century. His relationship to the earth, therefore, was established long before society developed its ever more complex technologies for separating human creatures from the rest of creation.

Throughout his young manhood, farming was largely the labor of muscle and bone, hoof and hand. The very first successful gasoline tractor was not manufactured until 1892. In 1907 there were a mere 600 tractors in the entire United States.

Thanne can remember the years before her father purchased his first John Deere in the late forties. She watched him plowing behind draft horses, steady beasts with hooves the size of the little girl's head.

"Prince," the farmer called them, and "Silver."

Often it was Ruthanne's task to lead them to water. And this is why she remembers the time and the chore so well: it frightened the child to walk between two such massive motors of rolling hide, her head below their necks. The quicker she went, the quicker they took their mighty paces, until she thought she could never stop them, and they would fly headlong into the pond, all three!

Her father, however, commanded them mutely with a gesture, with a cluck and a tap of the bridle. Silent farmer. Silent, stolid horses. They were for him a living, companionable power. And when Martin and his horses spent days plowing fields—moving with huffs and clomps and the ringing of chains, but with no explosions of liquid fuel—their wordless communication became community. The farmer never worked alone. He was never isolated. And if the dog named Rex ran beside them, then there were four who could read and obey the rhythms of creation, four creatures, therefore, who dwelt in communion with their Creator.

Ah, what a woven whole that world was! How the picture stirs my yearning—and my sadness too, if I could not enter the peace the farmer knows!

Horses plowed. ("Hup, Silver. Hup!") Horses mowed. Horses pulled the rake that laid the alfalfa in windrows to dry—giving Martin's fields the long, strong lines of a darker green that looked, from the road, like emotion wreathed in an ancient face.

And when the hay was dry, horses pulled a flat wagon slowly by the windrows while one man forked the hay up to another who stood on the wagon. This second man caught the bundles neatly on his own fork, then flicked them into an intricate cross-arrangements on the wagon, building the hay higher and tighter, climbing his work as he did, climbing so high that when the horses pulled the wagon to the barn, the man on his haystack could stare dead-level into the second-story windows of the farmhouse. Then horses pulled the rope that, over a metal wheel, hoisted the hay to the loft in the barn.

Martin and his neighbors made hayricks of the overflow. They thatched the tops against rain and the snow to come. The work caused a gritty dust, and the dust caused a fearful itch on a summer's day. But the work and the hay—fodder for the fall and the winter ahead—were a faithful obedience to the seasons and the beasts, Adam and Eve responsible for Eden. Martin Bohlmann knew that!

He milked the cows before sunrise. There was a time when he sat on a stool with his cheek against their warm flanks in winter. Cows would swing their heads around to gaze at him. He pinched the teats in the joint of his thumb and squeezed with the rest of his hand, shooting a needle *spritz* into the pail between his ankles. He rose. He lifted the full pail and sloshed its blue milk into the can; then he carried the cans, two by two, outside.

The winter air had a bite. His boots squeaked on the crusted snow as he lugged the cans to the milk house. The dawn was grey at the eastern horizon, the white earth ghostly, the cold air making clouds at the farmer's nostrils—and someone might say that he, alone in his barnyard, was lonely. He wasn't, of course; he was neither lonely nor alone. His boots still steamed with the scent of manure; his cheek kept the oil of the cattle's flanks; the milk and the morning were holy. They were—the very harmony of them was—manifestation of the Creator. And the work was nothing more or less than Martin's obedience. Of which is peace.

1991–1995:

When Thanne and I moved from Evansville in the southeast corner of Indiana to Valparaiso in the northeast, I was granted the chance to fulfill a personal yearning—a life-long yearning, to tell the truth, but one made ever more intense by the farms of eastern Illinois. I wanted in some modest way to live the farmer's life. We sought more than a lot and a house, therefore. Thanne and I went looking for land. Today we own twenty-four acres, fields and woods, a tool shed, a barn.

Martin himself had retired before we moved to this place; but we were closer to him now, could visit and talk with greater frequency. And I could focus my questions upon practical problems and solutions of my own small farm.

I have learned! In these latter years, I've come to understand the thing I once could only admire.

So, then: in the spring of 1992, I became the owner of a John Deere 5000 series farm tractor. It pulls at the power of forty horses, more than enough to handle the work I do, light plowing, disking. I drag timber from the woods to cut and split for firewood; I mow the broader fields, stretch fence, chip tree limbs, grade the ground and haul earth and stone and sand—all with my little Deere. The machine is perfectly suited to the cultivation of our modest crops, berry bushes, hickory and walnut trees, strawberry hills, scattered stands of apple trees, a sizable vegetable garden.

For decades before our relocation north, my family and I had lived in the inner city. We were hedged in on every side. True safety (or so it seemed to me) existed only within the walls of our house. I lived in suspicion of strangers. My children's new friends—the boy-type friends especially—might-could bring the threat that I could not protect against. After nightfall folks regularly gathered across the street from our house to drink, gamble, smoke dope. I *slept* tense.

I drove my car with such distracted anxiety that Evansville Police Officers knew me by sight: the pastor with a rap sheet. Well, I was not felonious; but I'd gathered my share of driving tickets and accident reports.

Once we came to the land, however, and once I'd learned to listen to its rhythms, I've felt a dear sense of expansion—yes, and the beginning of peace: I plant and pick, harrow and harvest generous crops in their due seasons.

My tractor is nothing like the modern behemoths that cut swaths as wide as avenues through dustier fields, machines wearing double tires on every wheel, pulling several gangs of plows and disks and harrows at once, while the operator sits bunkered in an air-conditioned cab, watching the tracks of his tires in a television monitor.

Me, I take the weather on my head. I mow at the width of six feet. And mine is but a two-bottom plow.

But Martin's wisdom makes of small things true sufficiency.

Summer, the late '40s:

My father-in-law purchased his first tractor—a John Deere exactly as green as mine, but smaller and less powerful—at the only price he could afford, something less that two hundred dollars.

"Billig," he judged the sale, which could be translated from the German as "Cheap," but which in his mouth meant, "Such a deal!" He bought the tractor used from one of his neighbors. The machine wasn't even two years old, but it kept stalling, driving the neighbor crazy. In the barnyard, in the field, pulling a wagon or plowing, the tractor would quit and refuse to produce the spark for starting again, however hard the poor man cranked.

That farmer figured he was selling aggravation.

Martin, on the other hand, sought to buy a sturdy servant, not only with his cash but also with his spirit. The dollars bought the cold equipment; but patience and peace bought time to examine it with complete attention, his mind untroubled; and mother-wit brought the tool to life again.

In those days tractors used a magneto generator. My father-in-law opened it and discovered a loose washer inside. The washer had shifted whenever the tractor bumped over rough ground, shorting the coils and killing the engine. Martin simply removed that washer. Thereafter he had a dependable tool for as long as ever he farmed. It was there when I came courting his daughter. It was there when he finally retired at the age of seventy and was forced to auction off his farming equipment.

Autumn 1993:

Near the western boundary of my acreage, the land descends to a low draw through which my neighbor's fields drain their runoff waters. For several years, the only way I could get back to the woods—and to the writing studio I'd built there—was through that draw. But every spring the thaw and the thunderstorms turned it into a wide stretch of sucking mud.

In order to correct my problem (to me it *was* a "problem") I laid a culvert west-and-west over the lowest section of the draw, then hired a man with a diesel earth shovel to dig a pond on the east side, then to pile that dirt over my culvert. I built a high bank, a dry pathway wide enough to take the weight of my tractor. I seeded it with grass, and the grass grew rich and green. Had God given us dominion over the earth? Well, I congratulated myself for having dominated this little bit of earth.

Congratulated myself and used this elevated path, that is, until the following spring, when severe storms caused such floods that the earth broke and my metal culvert was washed backward and submerged in the pond.

I tried again. I paid several college students to help me re-set the culvert, re-dig and re-pile the earth upon it. I walled the mouth of the culvert with rock and stone in order to teach the water where to go. I re-seeded the whole, yes. Yes, and during the summer months I watched miserably as little runnels of water found their ways beneath the culvert. By spring these runnels had scoured out caves, and the caves caused the culvert to slump, so that my draw returned to its first state as if it had never been anything else: primal mud.

When Martin came to visit, I showed him my new John Deere. He described for me the pattern for efficient plowing, then told me the story I've recounted above, about his own first tractor. We walked slowly across my back field. I took him to my failed culvert. That's what I called it while we stood by soupy pond: "Failed."

Martin turned bodily and looked at the fields west of mine. Even in old age his cheeks still bunched beneath his eyes. He seemed ever to maintain a private smiling. And his nose! That wondrous blade looked Navaho, though the man was German, through and through.

He turned back again and looked down at the flood-torn earth at our feet.

"Take your time," he said to me as if the last two years had been no time at all. "You've got the time," he said. Martin was himself ninety-three years old, and I but forty-nine. Yes, from his vantage I had whole quantities of time.

Finally he raised his eyes to mine and said, "Ask the water what *she* wants, then give her a new way to do it."

My John Deere 5000 makes a low muttering sound. At full throttle it emits a commanding growl. But its voice is muffled, modern.

Martin's first tractor uttered that steady *pop-pop-pop-pop* which, when it called across the fields to the farmhouse, revealed the essential vastness of the earth and all skies.

Pop-pop-pop-pop! Thanne recalls how she would step outside the farmhouse with her father's lunch, cock her eye and listen for that *pop-pop,* then follow the sound to find the farmer. She ran between cornstalks as high as her waist, the flat leaves nodding, whispering, slapping her legs as she passed them by. In the lunchbox were thick beef sandwiches, some cookies, coffee and two toothpicks. Always the toothpicks for her father at the end of his meals.

Pop-pop-pop-pop, and suddenly the child would come out on high ground and catch sight of her father in the distance, mowing between the solitary cottonwoods, creeping the low and golden land beneath the white cumulus giants striding the blue sky above. *How tiny,* little Ruthanne would think to herself, unable to distinguish her father's features. *How little he is:* one man on a tractor, far away.

But *How peaceful,* think I to myself, in spite of Martin's littleness in the universe. And: *How completely peaceful is this man!*

For during these last years, I've learned to know the nature of his peace, that it is not in spite of his smallness. Verily, it is *in* the smallness, as long as his is smallness under God.

For Martin Bohlmann, the sweet admission of his personal limitations was ever the beginning of wisdom. Only in knowing oneself as *created* can one know God as *Creator.* Otherwise, striving to be in control of our lives, the true Controller must feel like an adversary of massive and terrible force.

I have despised the limits on my own existence, and in that despite have suffered perpetual tensions, seen enemies everywhere. Why, the common act of driving a car can become a contest of mortal consequence. For the streets are battlegrounds, aren't they?

But Martin dwelt in patience and in peace.

Faith and trust and farming were all the same to him. He read the weather as humbly as he read the Bible, seeking what to obey. My father-in-law was an obedient man. This is the crux of the matter: his *obedience* was the source of his peace, because the one whom he obeyed was God of all, and by obedience Martin became one with all that God had made, as powerful himself and as infinite as the Deity with whom he was joined.

Daily the farmer did more than just read and interpret the rhythms of creation (though these he *did* do, these he *had* to do, for his vocation depended upon such readings, or the farm would fail). As Prince and Silver heeded their master's mute commands, so the farmer also obeyed the natural signs of the Creator, entering into communion with God Almighty.

So here was Martin's peace: not in striving for greatness but in recognizing who is truly great. And this was his peace: by a glad humility to do the will of the Creator.

And so this was Martin's peace as well: to bear the image of God into creation.

> Have you not known? Has it not been told you from the beginning? It is he who sits above the circle of the earth, and its inhabitants are like grasshoppers; who stretched out the heavens like a curtain and spreads them like a tent to dwell in. . . .
>
> Lift up your eyes on high and see: who created these? He who brings out their host by number, calling them all by

name; by the greatness of his might, and because he is strong in power, not one is missing.

April 30, 1995:

No, but one *is* missing! Martin is missing. My father-in-law himself. He is gone. This man is dead.

I'm driving south on Interstate 57 with a clenched jaw and stark knuckles. Angry. Anxious, really. It's nearly nighttime. South of Kankakee the Illinois farmland stretches east and west of me. More than I seeing it, I feel the cultivated earth as a swelling tide, a heaving of massy weight as of an ocean. It will fall on me soon, and I will drown.

I am about forty-five minutes from the funeral home in Watseka where Thanne is, and my children. And Martin in a box.

I'm driving at sixty-five miles per hour precisely. The speed limit. Cars rip past me, fire-eyed enemies, each one triumphing over me in my pickup. This particular obedience is not my habit. But I'm torn between desires to be with Thanne and *never* to be near the casket of my father. So I'm going at a grim, calculated slowness.

Death and the empty skies consume me now.

I hate this pickup truck! A beaten '84 Chevy S–10, the seat's too low and too hard. It wasn't made for distance driving. My back is killing me. Oh, God, I want to howl! To howl at *you!*

Because all our human limitations may be made easy in obedience—all, Sir, but this last one: death!

I gnash my teeth. I roll down my window and weep with the frustration of it all. *Martin is not here! I can do nothing about that!* This single, final limit makes every other limitation insupportable! And God's infinitude becomes my hell, for it makes my smallness burn like a flesh afire.

I have already left the Interstate. I'm driving east on highway 24, approaching state highway 49. The night is hugely black, endlessly empty above my little vehicle, though once I took the farmer's daughter for rides on county roads nearby, and then the nights were filled with delicious mystery.

I had a VW convertible in those days. When the nightwind grew chilly, Ruthanne would draw her knees up to her breast and pull the sweatshirt down over all to her ankles. That tender gesture stole my heart; her easy intimacy made me a citizen of the night and all that countryside. But there was no death in those days.

The parking lot is full. So I pull out again. I park on a side street and walk back. The funeral home spills light from various windows. I can hear a hubbub within.

I enter at the side of the building, artificial light, heat, a human humidity.

In the hallway I hang up my jacket. With slow steps I move to the viewing room. Martin's name and the dates that round his life are on a framed placard: 1900 to 1995. There is a birthday and a deathday.

I shift my sight to the room and look through the doorway. Many people are sitting. I recognize Thanne's sisters, her brothers.

And then, astonishingly, here is Thanne standing directly before me, looking up into my face.

My wife, my wife: are we okay together?

Her countenance wears a pleasant expression. She has not been crying. She touches my cheek. This is how Thanne will remove dried patches of shaving cream. It's also how she indicates to me by feel what she sees by sight: *my* face does not wear a pleasant expression. Yes. I know how gaunt and anxious I am, my face and my spirit, both.

Thanne takes my hand.

"Come," she says gently. She leads me into the wide viewing room. People glance my way, acknowledge my arrival. They sit on folding chairs all around the walls. Others stand in knots of conversation.

There is the casket, at the far end surrounded by a jungle of flowers. It has the appearance of an altar in church. No one is near it now. We approach, still hand in hand. The room seems (can this be?) to hush a little. I feel a general expectancy. But my role among the Bohlmann's is of no greater stature than anyone else's. In fact, this hush tightens my stomach even more than it was. I don't like to be on display. No emotion could possibly be natural and easy under scrutiny.

But Thanne continues forward to the casket, drawing me with her.

Behind the casket's linen, I see that great sail of a nose now rise up. Yes, it is Martin whom I'm coming to see. Yes: and there is his cantankerous hair. Even in death those spikes will not lie down. His eyebrows, too, are great sprouts of hair. His eyes are closed. His bunchy cheeks are slightly rouged.

Suddenly Thanne lets a little giggle escape her lips. The sound of it tingles inside of me. *She's laughing?* But then I see the farmer's mouth, and I understand her immediately and completely. Sticking straight up from the corner of his lips, causing a little grin to pool there, is a toothpick, straight, bold, erect.

Thanne tries to whisper in my ear, "The mortician . . ."

But the whisper becomes a squeal: "Oh, Wally," she squeals with perfect clarity, "the mortician's mort*ified!*" And then she can't help it. She breaks out in laughter.

That laughter kills me. I mean, it kills my silly anger; and I glance at Thanne's bright, wet eyes and burst into laughter, too.

Martin doesn't move; but his face is not offended by the hilarity, and besides, he was never a talky man. And here are my children, gathering, grinning, all four of them. And now I know what the whole room was anticipating: my taking the last step, my joining them, too.

And so I know exactly what happened after lunch on Friday, April 18, 1995.

Martin Bohlmann, having finished his meal, popped a toothpick into his mouth. He wasn't about to read his devotions. Rather, he was about to *do* them, devoutly and well.

And though he'd mostly been bound to a wheelchair, the farmer got up nevertheless, and pushed that chair aside and strolled out the door and into the fields west of his dwellings. Twilight. Farther and farther west the old man walked, until he came to a place of pausing. He tucked his hands under the bib of coveralls and gazed extremest west and listened to the deepest rhythms of the universe.

Yes, and I know what happened then. In his own good time, Martin Bohlmann knelt on one knee and scooped up a handful of the black earth and brought it to his face and smelled in it its readiness for plowing and for planting.

A springtime breeze got up and blew. And when at last my father-in-law allowed the soil sift from his hands into the wind, why, it was himself that blew forth, ascending. Here was the dust of his human frame and the lightsome stuff of his spirit.

This, then, I know as well as I know any other thing: even his death was an obedience.

Martin died, therefore, in a perfect peace.

WHEN YOU GET THERE,
WAIT!

LITTLE ONE, are you afraid of the dark?

Is that why you grab my hand and press against me? Because you are frightened?

Well, if we were still in the city I would show you the places where good people live. I'd name them and describe their kindness. Then if we had trouble, we could walk to a door and knock and get help.

In the city I would tell you where the hospital is and how to avoid dark alleys and which streets are well-lit. Or else I would just take you home. . . .

But we're not in the city, are we? And dark is darker where no human lights are. Even the noises are foreign here: no human machinery, no cars, no trucks, no TV, or tapes, or radio.

Little one! You cling to my arm as though the touch itself will keep you from harm, as though I were a good strong guard; and yet you tremble!

Are you still so scared of the dark?

O sweetheart, if we were out in the country now I would teach you the goodness of God's creation, even at night. I'd show you the stars and tell you their tales till they became your friends: the giant Orion (three stars for his belt and three for his dagger), the seven sisters all in a bunch (called the Pleiades, even in Scripture), Cassiopeia (whose shape makes a bent W like my initial). I'd light the star of Bethlehem. I'd talk about the angels, "the hosts of heaven," until the night skies were crowded by kindly spirits and we were not lonely below them.

In the country I'd make you hear the wind; I'd teach you the breath of God therewith, the *spiritus Dei*. God, who made it, keeps it still. The Creator laughs at the bullfrog's burp and loves the mockingbird—melodies, melodies, all night long. The phantom flight of the owl, the cricket's chirrup, the wolf's exquisite, killing harmonies—all these you would hear as the handiwork of God, just as you yourself are God's good handiwork. And then, my dear, you would be consoled. . . .

But we're not in the country, are we?

Little one, you whimper with fear. You turn and you bury your face in my bosom. I hug you with all my strength, with all my love. I rock you and rock you and stroke your thin hair—but still you are scared of the dark.

O my dear heart! O my dear, if you were going blind, if *that* were the darkness into which you descended, I would teach you touching—and feeling itself would be your light.

I'd lift your fingers to my face and let you touch me from temple to chin. Brush my lashes. Brush my smiling eyes. Linger at my cheekbone. Take upon your fingertips my kisses. Then take my hand and let me walk you through the dark world till all its furniture becomes familiar to you.

But. . .but the blindness you suffer is worse than that, isn't it?

Baby, afraid of the dark! Scared of the prison the darkness shuts around you! Frightened because you are soon nowhere at all, in spaces invisible, endless, empty. . . .

O little one, we know what your darkness is, don't we?

It's old age. You have grown old. And now comes the deepest darkness of all: you are dying.

My little one, my darling! The dark is your departure. You are leaving this world altogether, going to that undiscovered country from whose bourn no traveler returns. Yes? Yes.

Yes, and my darkness is sorrow, because I must remain behind.

Hush, old hoary head. My best beloved, hush. Let me hold you a while. Cling to me as tightly as you please, and I will whisper the thoughts that occur to me now.

No. This is not some city through which we travel. Yet there is a city ahead of you. And you shall enter before I do. But I am coming, and then it shall be *you* who welcomes *me* and makes the streets of that place familiar to me.

Because you are dying in faith, my little one—you who always were but a pilgrim on this earth. You're finishing the trip begun by Baptism; you are entering a better country, that is, a heavenly country. Wherefore God is not ashamed to be called your God—for he hath prepared for you this city!

And when you arrive, you won't need me to show you around. God will meet you there. Alleys and highways, God will show you everything—but first he'll take from your vision the crust of old age, the terrors and the troubles of this present world: for God himself shall wipe all tears from your eyes; and there shall be no more death neither sorrow, nor crying anymore.

And no: the dark surrounding you now is not the countryside either, nor sky nor stars nor the woofings and bleats of God's creatures. It is, in fact, their absence, since you are passing away from all this.

Ah, but you go from creation to its Creator! You go to the God who conceived of Eden and Paradise and everything between the two. Better than the handiwork of God, dear heart, is God himself.

But yes: dying is a kind of blindness. It is preparation for deeper sight and dearest insight. Little one, this darkness is not because you cannot see, but because the world cannot *be* seen. The material world is becoming a shadow before you, so that the coming world (bright with divine reality) may not blind you at your arrival. That city is brighter than sunlight. It hath no need of the sun in it. For the glory of God doth lighten it, and the Lamb is the light thereof.

Hush, now. Close your eyes. Don't be afraid. I'll hold you with my lowly love till God receives you in his highest, most holy love. My darling, you are embarking through darkness on your best adventure. Only the start is scary. The rest is endlessly marvelous, eternally beautiful.

But when you get there, wait!

Turn around. Look back through the glorious light, and watch for me. I am coming, too.

MIZ LIL AND THE CHRONICLES OF GRACE
BRAND NEW EDITION

In *Miz Lil and the Chronicles of Grace*, a well-conceived unit of twelve beautifully told stories, anecdotes, and reminiscences evokes the experience of growing up American and living out a spiritual quest. Culled from Wangerin's childhood, adolescence, young adulthood, and his years as an inner-city pastor, the interwoven stories lend flesh, feeling, and immediacy to themes that are vital to every Christian. With a new Afterword by the author, *Miz Lil and the Chronicles of Grace* unfolds the moving story of a pastor and storyteller's career and the drama of his faith.
Softcover: 0-310-24169-3

LITTLE LAMB, WHO MADE THEE?
A BOOK ABOUT CHILDREN AND PARENTS

The stories, essays, prayers, and poems in *Little Lamb, Who Made Thee?* continue the themes the author began in *Ragman and Other Cries of Faith*. Here are children, teenagers, adults, and parents grappling with the deep realities of life. Painting with bold brushstrokes of human emotion and using a wise and gentle humor, Wangerin probes the relationships between children and their parents and what they have to show us about God and ourselves as his children. Like *Ragman*, this volume includes twelve new stories, fresh from the master storyteller's pen.
Softcover: 0-310-24826-4

RAGMAN AND OTHER CRIES OF FAITH
NEW AND EXPANDED EDITION

The interlocking stories in *Ragman and Other Cries of Faith* helped usher Walter Wangerin to prominence as a Christian writer. The opening chapter, "Ragman," remains one of Wangerin's most popular works and leads the reader into thirty-three other writings in a variety of styles. Ranging from the gently reflective to the incantatory, they are powerful, thought-provoking explorations of the meaning of faith, the person of Christ, the community of believers, and the individual servant of faith. Eleven new pieces are included in this definitive edition.
Softcover: 0-060-52614-9

EXPANDED EDITIONS OF *RAGMAN AND OTHER CRIES OF FAITH*; *LITTLE LAMB, WHO MADE THEE?* AND *MIZ LIL AND THE CHRONICLES OF GRACE* ALL IN ONE BOOK!

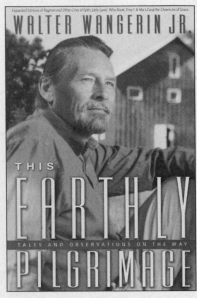

THIS EARTHLY PILGRIMAGE

TALES AND OBSERVATIONS ON THE WAY

Ragman and Other Cries of Faith; *Little Lamb, Who Made Thee?* and *Miz Lil and the Chronicles of Grace* are among Walter Wangerin Jr.'s earliest and best-loved books. Each is a multi-faceted jewel containing stories, essays, parables, prayers, and meditations, all bearing the mark of Wangerin's trademark poignancy and lyricism.

While the books stand on their individual merits, the author originally conceived them as an interlinking set—a trio that would together weave a complex and vivid tapestry of human experience and "story theology." In *This Earthly Pilgrimage*, these beloved Wangerin classics come together at last, along with brand new writings, in an omnibus that lets the reader trace the tapestry's threads from their source to their completion.

Hardcover: 0-310-24970-8

Pick up a copy today at your favorite bookstore!

GRAND RAPIDS, MICHIGAN 49530 USA

WWW.ZONDERVAN.COM

A SAINT'S TALE FOR MODERN READERS!

SAINT JULIAN
A NOVEL

WALTER WANGERIN JR.

A stunning spiritual tale about the life of the legendary Saint Julian, who as a cruel hunter in his youth is doomed to a tragic fate, but only through a lifelong learning to perform acts of charity and kindness does he find redemption in his encounter with Christ himself.

In this spiritual allegory, the young knight Julian is an avid—even voracious—hunter and sportsman. But his thrill at taking the lives of his prey becomes an obsession until he one day confronts a mystical deer that prophesies that Julian will murder his own parents. Terrified, Julian travels across the world to make a home for himself as far from his parents as possible. As fate has it, his parents search for him and his wife takes them into Julian's castle and lets them sleep in the master bedroom. Julian returns late at night, enters the bedroom, and thinking he has found his wife with a secret lover, murders them both.

Realizing that the prophecy has come true, Julian leaves home for a lifetime of wandering and seeking penance. Ultimately he becomes a ferryman at a dangerous river crossing. When an elderly leper shows up and makes unusual demands upon Julian's kindness and hospitality, Julian discovers—with his final breath—that the old leper is Jesus himself, come to absolve Julian of his sin.

Hardcover: 0-060-52252-6

Pick up a copy today at your favorite bookstore!

ZONDERVAN™

GRAND RAPIDS, MICHIGAN 49530 USA

WWW.ZONDERVAN.COM

AN INTIMATE PORTRAIT OF A COMPLEX INDIVIDUAL

PAUL
A NOVEL

WALTER WANGERIN JR.

Walter Wangerin brings us a dramatic, fictionalized retelling of the life of Paul based on biblical texts and extensive on-site research. Readers gain a new appreciation for the sacrifices of the apostles and the early believers and gain new insights into the life of the early church.

With vivid imagination and scholarly depth, award-winning author Walter Wangerin Jr. weaves together the history of the early church with the life story of its greatest apostle—Paul. Wangerin begins to unfold Paul's incredible life by imagining the childhood and early family life of a boy then called "Saul." A fierce prosecutor of Christians before his conversion, Paul never lost his fiery dedication, boldness, and strong personality. After his shocking encounter with God on the road to Damascus, he applied his formidable strengths to spreading the gospel. Wangerin deftly reveals Paul's character through each stage of his life, and enables us to see Paul the person, living and complex, viewed through the eyes of his contemporaries: Barnabas, James, Prisca, Seneca, and Luke. Paul's rich interaction and brilliant dialogue with friends and foes, leaders and slaves, Jews and Greeks, create a swift and intense historical drama around the man who spread the seed of the Gospel to the ends of the known world.

Hardcover: 0-310-21892-6

Softcover: 0-310-24316-5

Unabridged Audio Pages® Cassette: 0-310-23591-X

Pick up a copy today at your favorite bookstore!

ZONDERVAN™

GRAND RAPIDS, MICHIGAN 49530 USA

WWW.ZONDERVAN.COM

A TRUSTWORTHY GUIDE TO AN INTIMATE RELATIONSHIP WITH GOD

WHOLE PRAYER

SPEAKING AND LISTENING TO GOD

WALTER WANGERIN JR.

Award-winning author Walter Wangerin Jr. gracefully explores the dynamics of prayer—of speaking, of listening, of waiting, and of hearing God's voice. With luminous prose, he surveys the landscape of communication and communion with God—what whole prayer feels like, looks like, and sounds like. He points out that whole prayer is a circle, closed and complete. We pour out our hearts and minds to God, who listens as we do. Then we listen intently for his voice when he speaks. Wangerin encourages readers not to eliminate any part of the circle so we don't cut the conversation short.

Softcover: 0-310-24258-4

Pick up a copy today at your favorite bookstore!

ZONDERVAN™

GRAND RAPIDS, MICHIGAN 49530 USA

WWW.ZONDERVAN.COM

FOLLOW EVERY DETAIL LEADING TO THE BIRTH OF CHRIST

PREPARING FOR JESUS

MEDITATIONS ON THE COMING OF CHRIST, ADVENT, CHRISTMAS, AND THE KINGDOM

WALTER WANGERIN JR.

In this Advent and Christmas devotional, best-selling author Walter Wangerin Jr. takes the reader day-by-day through the major events and characters leading up to the birth of Jesus in 36 meditations.

In *Preparing for Jesus,* the author recreates verbal images of the events surrounding the Advent of Christ, offering a devotional journey into the heart of the Christmas season. Through rich detail and vivid images, these moving meditations make Christ's birth both intimate and immediate, allowing us to see Christmas from its original happening to its perennial recurrence in our hearts. *Preparing for Jesus* is sure to be a seasonal classic, treasured year after year.

Hardcover: 0-310-20644-8

Pick up a copy today at your favorite bookstore!

ZONDERVAN™

GRAND RAPIDS, MICHIGAN 49530 USA

WWW.ZONDERVAN.COM

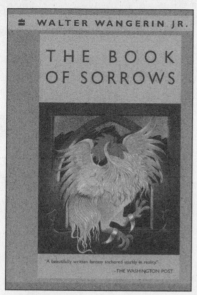

THE SEQUEL TO AN
AWARD-WINNING TITLE

The Book of Sorrows

WALTER WANGERIN JR.

This sequel to the award-winning *The Book of the Dun Cow* stands on its own as a powerful work of literature. In this absorbing, highly original fantasy, Chauntecleer, Pertelote, and the other familiar characters of the Coop struggle to piece together their shattered lives in the aftermath of the terrible conflict with the dreaded Wyrm. But their respite is short-lived: Into this struggling community, Wyrm again insinuates himself, with dire consequences for all. The reappearance of the dog Mundo Coni unveils a darker mystery yet—and the threat of a final horror when evil yields up its most devastating secrets. Told by a master storyteller, *The Book of Sorrows* is a taught and spellbinding tale that immerses readers in a variety of adventures—heroic, humorous, and touching—moving inexorably toward the final confrontation that decides the fate of the characters and their world. No one who reads it will remain unmoved. It explores the value and goodness of existence, the darker side of reality, and the qualities of love, kindness, courage, and hope that can transform even "this troublous existence." Here is fast-paced fantasy filled with richly drawn characters and gripping excitement, set against a colorful, fully realized world, and with depth of meaning that will draw readers back again and again to ponder the images long after the final battle is waged between the forces of life and death.

Softcover: 0-310-21081-X

Pick up a copy today at your favorite bookstore!

ZONDERVAN™

GRAND RAPIDS, MICHIGAN 49530 USA

WWW.ZONDERVAN.COM

A MOVING ALLEGORY OF
THE CHRISTIAN LIFE

THE ORPHEAN
PASSAGES

THE DRAMA OF FAITH

WALTER WANGERIN JR.

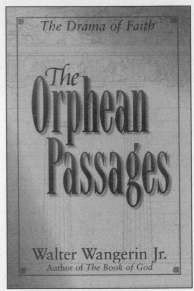

The Drama of Faith

The
Orphean
Passages

Walter Wangerin Jr.
Author of *The Book of God*

A remarkable weaving of faith, myth, and humanity from award-winning novelist Walter Wangerin Jr. "Faith," writes Walter Wangerin, is "a relationship with the living God enacted in this world." It is ever-changing and inherently dramatic. *The Orphean Passages* is Wangerin's compelling story of a Christian pastor's career and the drama of his faith. Interlaced with the classical myth of Orpheus and Eurydice, this daring and unconventional inquiry into Christian experience ranks among the most challenging of Wangerin's works. Wangerin sees in the ancient myth an extraordinary parallel of the twists and turns individuals follow in their journeys of faith. In the author's own present-day Reverend Orpheus, that parallel is vividly played out—rendering the modern story of one man both universal and timeless. *The Orphean Passages* asserts the truth of a legend that people of all times have experienced. It has the immediacy of a well-wrought novel, driving readers on to the surprising yet inevitable conclusion.

Softcover: 0-310-20568-9

Pick up a copy today at your favorite bookstore!

ZONDERVAN™

GRAND RAPIDS, MICHIGAN 49530 USA

WWW.ZONDERVAN.COM

HELP THE HURTING AND
YOURSELF THROUGH THIS
AMAZING BOOK

Mourning into Dancing

WALTER WANGERIN JR.

"Death doesn't wait till the ends of
our lives to meet us and to make an
end," says Walter Wangerin. "Instead,
we die a hundred times before we die;
and all the little endings on the way are
like a slowly growing echo of the final BANG!" Yet out of our many losses,
our "little deaths," comes a truer recognition of life. It is found in our
relationships with ourselves, with our world, with others, and with our
Creator. This is the dancing that can come out of mourning: the hope of
restored relationships. *Mourning into Dancing* defines the stages of grief,
names the many kinds of loss we suffer, shows how to help the grief-
stricken, gives a new vision of Christ's sacrifice, and shows how a loving
God shares our grief. We learn from this book that the way to dancing is
through the valley of mourning—that grief is a poignant reminder of the
fullness of life Christ obtained for us through his resurrection. In the
words of writer and critic John Timmerman, *Mourning into Dancing*
"could well be the most important book you ever read."

Softcover: 0-310-20765-7

Pick up a copy today at your favorite bookstore!

ZONDERVAN™

GRAND RAPIDS, MICHIGAN 49530 USA

WWW.ZONDERVAN.COM

A MASTER STORYTELLER DRAMATIZES THE ENTIRE BIBLE!

The Book of God

THE BIBLE AS A NOVEL

WALTER WANGERIN JR.

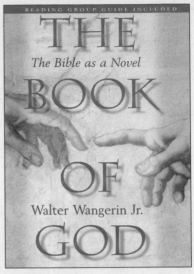

The Bible as a Single, Powerful Story

Here is the entire story of the Bible, narrated by master storyteller Walter Wangerin Jr. Reading like a great historical novel, *The Book of God* dramatizes the sweep of biblical events, making the men and women of this ancient book come alive in vivid detail and dialogue. From Abraham wandering in the desert to Jesus teaching the multitudes on a Judean hillside, *The Book of God* follows the biblical story in chronological order. Imaginative yet meticulously researched, *The Book of God* offers a sweeping history that stretches across thousands of years and hundreds of lives, in cultures foreign and yet familiar in their common humanity. History and fact take on personality and warmth. Wangerin makes the places where the events of the Bible took place come to life in the imagination. Wangerin helps you understand what it was like for each person to be caught up in the events of a particular time and place—a time and place where the eternal God somehow reached out and touched ordinary men and women. *The Book of God* is no ordinary book. Written by a born storyteller, it is the magnum opus of one of the most respected and beloved authors of our time.

Hardcover: 0-310-20005-9

Softcover: 0-310-22021-1

Special Edition: 0-310-23612-6

Unabridged Audio Pages® Cassette: 0-310-20422-4

Video: 0-310-21068-2

Pick up a copy today at your favorite bookstore!

GRAND RAPIDS, MICHIGAN 49530 USA

WWW.ZONDERVAN.COM

A PERFECT DEVOTIONAL FOR
THE LENTEN SEASON

RELIVING THE
PASSION

MEDITATIONS ON THE
SUFFERING, DEATH, AND
THE RESURRECTION OF
JESUS AS RECORDED IN
MARK

WALTER WANGERIN JR.

No story has more significance than this: the death and resurrection of Jesus. But somehow the oft-repeated tale of Christ's Passion can become too familiar, too formalized, for us to experience its incredible immediacy. The meditations in *Reliving the Passion,* which received a Gold Medallion award in 1993, follow the story as given in the gospel of Mark—from the moment when the chief priests plot to kill Jesus to the Resurrection. But these readings are more than a recounting of events; they are an imaginary reenactment, leading the reader to re-experience the Passion or perhaps see it fully for the very first time. As only a great storyteller can, Walter Wangerin takes his readers inside the story of Christ's passion. *Reliving the Passion* translates the events into the realm of feeling, image, and experience. In richly personal detail, Wangerin helps us recognize our own faces in the streets of Jerusalem; breathe the dark air of Golgotha; and experience, as Mary and Peter did, the bewilderment, the challenge, and the ultimate revelation of knowing the man called Jesus.

Hardcover: 0-310-75530-1

Pick up a copy today at your favorite bookstore!

GRAND RAPIDS, MICHIGAN 49530 USA

WWW.ZONDERVAN.COM